THE PIE GUYS

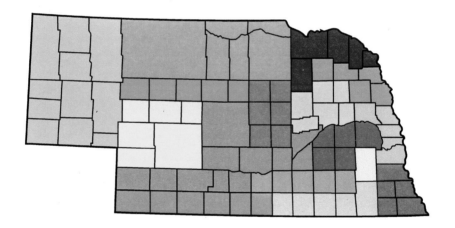

The Pie Guys: A Nebraska Story
by Joe Coleman
ISBN: 978-0-578-29408-7

Published by and photos courtesy of Joe Coleman
Cover and book layout by Aaron Grauer
Printed by Firespring - Lincoln, NE

To my wife Anna, who never did anything but support this whole thing. That included putting up with me bringing home extra slices, asking her to judge them, and then telling her she was judging them wrong. Babe, you're incredible, and I love you.

Special thanks to Aaron Grauer for his ability and willingness to make this as presentable as possible (not an easy task with what he was given). You rock, my friend.

And of course, to AJ and Charlie. This was a highlight in my life, and it wouldn't have been the same with anyone else.

Why?

I came to expect laughter and confusion when I would tell people "My friends and I are eating a piece of Pie in every Nebraska county." The response never changed. "What made you do this?" Despite having years to prepare an adequate answer, I never made progress. "No reason" was my usual offering, but something in me knew it must have gone deeper.

The idea for what would affectionately become known as "Piebraska" came into being around 2008. Originally the goal was to eat all 93 pieces in one fell swoop. I figured eating five or six pieces a day for two to three weeks straight was reasonable. I honestly thought that. Forget that five pieces of your average Pie would fill most of one's daily caloric intake, and you wouldn't feel much like eating anything else with that kind of overload. But I was young, and health was the least of my concerns. As a college student, the only missing ingredients were time and money, both of which would be quite helpful for this kind of thing. A very logical and reasonable friend of mine (don't tell him I said so) suggested doing the trip in multiple legs, broken up and spaced out. Years of my shaming him followed for having the audacity to stomp on my dreams of the ultimate Nebraska road trip — until a decade later when I did exactly that.

Thankfully I wasn't alone, and every bit of this journey was shared with the only two guys who were brave (and dumb) enough to embark on this with me, AJ and Charlie. I won't go into it all here, but there are a few things you should know about these fine gentlemen.

I met AJ in the early-2000's when we worked our first job together in a local produce department. AJ is the kind of person up for anything. For instance: in answering a Craigslist ad, he now walks multiple times per week with a total stranger who requested simply that, to have a companion to help him stay active. We've lived together, played in a Heavy Metal band together, and have now eaten a lot of Pie together.

Charlie is "Mr. Cool" (don't tell him I said so), as laid back as any human on this planet. I met him through AJ, who's known him since grade school. AJ and I had an apartment lease running out when he suggested we both move into Charlie's place. I met Charlie on moving day, and that was that. I'm not even sure he knew I was coming until I showed up with a bed. He didn't seem to care, and here we are well over a decade later. I should also mention that beyond what you obviously know from his inclusion here, Charlie really has a sweet tooth. For instance: the man drinks a lot of Coke (a lot of Coke). For a birthday years ago, we got him a pallet full of the stuff (literally, a rickety wooden pallet from a grocery store stacked four feet high in our kitchen). It was gone in two months.

What This Book Is, and What It Isn't

I must admit I had no intention of writing about this in any way when the idea came to life. It still wasn't my goal after it began. Sure, we'd keep a list of where we'd been, take some photos and discuss our favorites, but nothing further. There were no delusions of grandeur here, we just wanted to eat Pie and have a good time. That core of the trip never changed, but after I excitedly returned home from our first weekend excursion and couldn't stop telling stories of the day to family and friends, I was repeatedly urged to write everything down. Still hesitant for some time, I just couldn't see the end result of my writing being of interest to a stranger. I had a cheap camera that didn't take professional photos, I'd never written anything close to a book in my life, and I couldn't convince myself there was a real story to be told in it all. I still wonder, but as you're now finding out the hard way, I did decide to write it down. No, this isn't the part where I write the obligatory blurb about how traveling through small towns in the Midwest held a romanticism that re-shaped my very existence. I'm not qualified to make that statement even if it were true (which it might be). I'm from Lincoln, a big city as far as Nebraska is concerned, so these trips were a definite departure from daily life, and I loved every bit of it. But I don't think I'm ready to say outright and eloquently how this deviation from my routine has affected me. I've had more fun than I can say, and just hope more people do the same or similar and tell me what it did for them. In the meantime, this will have to serve as my best attempt to get it all down in one place, and maybe the "why" will become evident when someone smarter than me explains what exactly we accomplished.

The one thing I'm pretty sure we can claim is that this hasn't been done before. I've seen impressive documents of journeys with beautiful photographs, extensive research, and a way with words to make an experience feel as if every reader had lived it. I'll come right out and say that at least two of those elements will likely be lacking in the forthcoming pages, and I'm okay with that (I'm holding out hope that I can rouse something from inside whoever decides to continue). This trip required no expertise or (extensive) research, and that's the main reason why I think telling this story works. It's relatable, and can be done by anyone willing to simply move and eat with an open mind and mouth. If it does nothing else, I hope it inspires people to take what might seem ordinary and do something new and exciting with it. I can't tell you what we did was incredible or profound, because I'm pretty sure it wasn't. We may have found the best Pie in Nebraska, or maybe not. The only thing I'm sure of is that it was all worth it, and what else matters?

The Rules

Whatever this was, it wasn't exactly what you'd call scientific. Maybe it was due to this harsh reality that we felt the need to overly complicate some of its most basic points. What else can you do when you're driving hundreds of miles to eat a few slices but argue about every aspect of this seemingly frivolous venture?

First things first, the main objective once underway was to make sure we ate as many different kinds of Pie as possible. This wasn't a journey to find the best Apple Pie in Nebraska or anything like that. It wasn't nearly that focused. This may lead you to the reasonable conclusion that we won't be telling you definitively where the best place to eat Pie in the state is (although it certainly helped form some very strong opinions). To feel well rounded, variety and random chance were most often the themes of the day, and we let the cards fall where they may (this will make more sense very soon).

The baseline was simple: If there were three options at any stop, then all three were tried (by different participants, since we decided that exactly one kind should be tried per person). But who gets first pick? Initially, we intended to leave it to a coin flip, but how best to win between three people? The trickle-down coin flip (is that a thing?) was flawed, so we moved to a roll of the dice.

Unfortunately, we thought of this mid-journey and couldn't find a die along the way (at more than one roadside stop we even looked for a cheap board game to do the trick, but Yahtzees and the like were out of stock). Luckily for us, Charlie fancies himself a card shark or something, and always has a deck on hand. So cards it was! Discomfort and childish digs always being the name of the game, here's how they fell; AJ got the Ace of Clubs (because his favorite color is red), Charlie the Ace of Hearts (because he wanted the Ace of Diamonds) and I got the Ace of Diamonds (to spite Charlie). The Ace of Spades was off the table (RIP Lemmy). But who would draw the card? Surely no one man was to be trusted with such a monumental task that could so easily be tampered with, so it was decided the cards would be laid out at each location for our server to blindly choose.

The hand of fate

Without further ado, here's where everything sat after the dust settled on our first outing:

- The Pie must be acquired and eaten in the same county.

- If there are three or more options at any stop, no two participants can have the same kind.

- Whoever's card is drawn by the server gets first pick. The second pick goes to whoever wins a coin flip, executed by whoever's card was chosen.

- For second pick the oldest participant is always heads in the coin flip.

- If a stop has only one piece of Pie in total, additional stop options in the county

4

are explored. If none are found or available, that piece is cut into equal thirds to be tried by each participant.

- If a stop has exactly two total pieces of the same kind of Pie, additional stop options in the county are explored. If none are found or available, the two pieces are each cut into thirds and two pieces (2/3 of a total piece) are taken by each participant.

- If a stop has exactly two total pieces of two different kinds of Pie, additional stop options in the county are explored. If none are found or available, a coin is flipped to see which of the two options is chosen for all and is subsequently cut into thirds to be tried by each participant (this is the only scenario where a type of Pie is left uneaten with three or less options, so no one participant eats more than any other, and also to not have anybody eat two different kinds of Pie on the same stop. That would be madness).

- If exactly two kinds of Pie are available, the card drawn still determines first pick, followed by the coin flip. The winner of the coin flip can choose either Pie as well. If the winner of the coin flip chooses the same type as the first, the third person must eat the remaining type of Pie. If the winner of the coin flip chooses differently than the first, the third person can choose either type.

- If there is a variety of Pie that has not been tried up to that point during Pie-braska, then it must be chosen before any other option that has been tried.

- All ratings must be completed prior to the next Pie being eaten. No altering of ratings is allowed at a later time.

The Ratings

This was the real crux of the trip, and what filled a lot of our time on the road with endless debate between stops. If you're one of the kind souls who baked, prepared, served or directed us in any way toward Pie on this trip, please don't take any less than stellar rating personally. The reality is that not all Pies are created equal, yet some of our favorite stops of the tour had nothing to do with the integrity of the Pie anyhow. There are other things in life besides Pie (God forbid), and trying to eat it everywhere we could was a great way to prove that sentiment, but debating its merit is VERY fun!

It must also be noted that all individual ratings listed after each leg are extremely subjective and personal, and based in no way on any widely accepted professional standards (we're full blown amateurs). We used the following framework:

Filling	**Visual**
Consistency; Content; Texture; (Proportional) Amount	Presentation of the single slice

Crust	**Taste**
How well-baked or prepared; Texture	I don't need to explain this one, right?

Each of the four categories receives a rating from 1-5 based on what each of us feels to be ideal, making a 20-pointer the perfect Pie. Let's eat!

The chariot awaits

AN ADVENTURE 10 YEARS IN THE MAKING

2/24/18 ——————————————— **197 Miles**

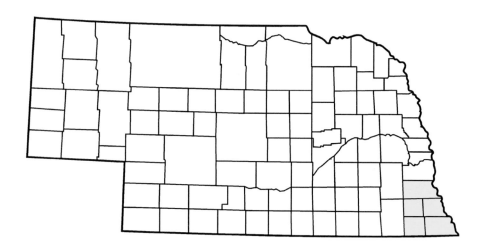

The excitement was palpable after a decade of anticipation. The Pie tour was finally underway, and the energy began to build leading up to that Saturday in February. As the date got closer the weather got worse, and after being warned to delay our departure by anyone close enough to care... we decided to go anyway.

All faith was put in my trusty 1998 Toyota Corolla, which barely made it through the early morning ice hell. After AJ and I escaped unscathed from the Toyota's full 360 at Cotner and O St, we eventually made it to Charlie's, traveling roughly 1 mph. Pie-braska was on.

After passing the Otoe County sign and having a long debate regarding how best to catalog this trip, it was decided to have a Pie-braska county chart signed at each stop by a cook or server. It didn't take long after landing at Mary's in Nebraska City to figure out that disrupting its namesake while she made breakfast for a room full of hungry folks would be unwise (our server formally warned us). So, without daring to do so ourselves, she offered to take the chart to the kitchen window for us. The next thing heard loudly by everyone occupying Mary's at the time was an unhappy voice from the kitchen exclaiming "Pie-braska?! I've never heard of that!" The chart returned unsigned. The server also elected not to sign, presumably due to being under tyrannical rule, so getting 93 signatures was immediately out of the question. Despite this bumpy beginning, the Pie was fine. But boy, what a breakfast sandwich Mary makes. Just ask Charlie!

After Mary's we seemed to gain interest from others about our strange journey. Whether we said something or not, we were clearly oozing with child-like excitement (well... I was anyway), getting asked multiple times what it was we were up to. At Nemaha County's Metro Cafe on the main street of Auburn, Charlie's lack of proper Pie etiquette spawned the necessity for the drawing of cards moving forward. After our collective joy upon seeing the Caramel Apple option, he immediately ordered the piece for himself without consultation. Luckily, any ill will from this action (there was plenty) quickly subsided after seeing the awe-inspiring selection at Six Mile Cafe on Hwy 75 in Richardson County. With upwards of 15 choices, we were each allowed to try Pies we'd never had or heard of before, including our first of what we hoped would be many Sour Cream Raisins.

At Frazier's Cafe in Tecumseh however, we had some issues, mostly for reasons beyond the control of anyone in Johnson County. After eating three pieces of Pie and a meal each in a short time span, we had to put our rally caps on. It didn't help that Charlie was denied his choice of Pie twice after they ran out, each time causing the waitress to return one minute later and comically erase his choice from the white board's dessert menu, eventually forcing him into a Cherry he never wanted. His gut was apparently right. So, with heavy stomachs we said goodbye to the cat casually walking out of Frazier's kitchen, which surprised only us, and departed for our final stop.

The small village of Lewiston in Pawnee County gave us Jeannie's Place, which capped the day beautifully. Hers is an actual residence where dinners are prepared and served by appointment only in her expansive dining area next to her impressive and open kitchen. When I spoke with Jeannie on the phone a week earlier she was more than willing to let us drop in mid-afternoon before that Saturday's planned dinner. When we knocked on the side door it didn't take long for us to be warmly greeted by her asking, "Are you my Pie eaters?" We were welcomed in, stepped over another cat, and sat with Jeannie for a good hour while two Pies baking in the oven filled the room with a kind of joy we hadn't yet experienced.

We entered Jeannie's a bit weary, yet her Pecan and Strawberry Rhubarb Pies straight out of the oven won us over with ease (it didn't hurt that she added a scoop of homemade ice cream to each piece without warning). This final stop was the clear highlight of the day, even while facing some solid competition. I wonder if the high marks weren't affected by the magnificent surroundings, but in the end, it doesn't really matter. This was the clearest indication on day one that this journey would be much less about finding the best Pie than it would be about experiencing something we couldn't plan for. Fortunately, Jeannie's Pies were phenomenal, so no separation between taste and experience was necessary. We also managed to get our story into the Pawnee Republican, our first local newspaper. We were told by Jeannie as we left that the editor would be happy to print something other than an obituary. It's reassuring to know our story rivals the dead.

QUOTES OUT OF CONTEXT

"My 50/50 chance has more variance
of chance with the coin flip due to
multiple flips." - AJ

"Can't eat every place out of
Pie and home." - Joe

THINGS WE LEARNED

The greatness of bacon is a hotly contested issue.

AJ wants to be just like Joe.

SPOTLIGHT:
Jeannie's Place
Lewiston, Pawnee County

Jeannie Tegtmeier's operation is one of a kind. She describes a trip there as "going to Grandma's house." This could be easily overlooked in other circumstances, where the phrase "just like mom used to make" is one we've all gotten used to hearing about a great many places that serve items nothing like our moms used to make. But when you walk into Jeannie's Place, it's hard to stress how true this sentiment is. You really will be sitting in grandma's kitchen and dining room, and that's something she finds very natural. There's no traditional menu, Jeannie just covers the table with serving dishes and bowls filled with old-fashioned home cooking, making your time there feel like Thanksgiving dinner. Serving her customers this way is something she says was "learned through osmosis."

Growing up on a farm just a few miles south of Lewiston, Jeannie was always around cooking. Her mother was a great cook and baker, traits she acquired through years of working alongside her. There wasn't a day where they weren't cooking for the family or hired hands who were put to work, so doing this for large groups came naturally. After college she became a teacher herself, but never lost her talents in the kitchen. She was still a mainstay at the family farm, helping out after hours and significantly more in the summer. At some point along the way, the idea struck her that "maybe people would pay me to do this." In 2010, after retiring from teaching, she decided to give it a whirl. She added onto the dining room of the home she'd lived in since 1989 and opened for business. Her place has since become a staple in the small town of Lewiston, bringing groups in each week for communal meals.

Jeannie has stayed around Lewiston her whole life because of kind people and her church. The community is important to her, and she's become part of its fabric in a new and meaningful way in the past decade. Lewiston lies between Pawnee City and Beatrice, making it a convenient stop for many who travel through the southeastern corner of the state. There's a lovely bed and breakfast in Steinauer, the Convent House, which comes with Jeannie's highest recommendation for travelers (where they can also marvel at the town's historic Catholic Church). And while it sits just over the western county line in Gage, there is a towering limestone barn in nearby Filley, built in 1874 by the town's founder Elijah Filley, earning a spot on the National Register of Historic Places.

If the wide open spaces and modest attractions aren't enough for you to warrant a detour, rest assured that Jeannie's is worth the trip all by itself. Come for the fried chicken, or to sample multiple homemade Pies that she prepares for every gathering (out of ten on the roster, her favorite of which is the Sour Cream Peach). While you're there you can play a tune on the grand piano that still sits in the dining room where she used to give lessons, or bring your kids along to play with the chickens seen just outside the new addition's window (or take a stroll with them yourself). The welcoming atmosphere is one that gives Jeannie great pride, which she recounted in one of her favorite memories since opening. After recently hosting a birthday party, a note came in the mail that read, "Thank you for the homey atmosphere."

THE REGULAR:
Shirley Malone

"Whatever she makes, it's gonna be good." Those were Shirley's first words when I asked her about Jeannie's Place. She's been a regular since day one, and their roots go back further than that. Shirley is from the nearby village of Burchard, where she tries to round up a carload of her friends every Tuesday afternoon to head to Jeannie's, where fried chicken and Pie are routinely featured. "We've always known her," Shirley tells me, noting their kids grew up together, and that Jeannie was always a mainstay at the local 4H gatherings, where everyone would wait anxiously to see which Pies she'd brought for the group on any given day. Shirley's brothers and sisters started coming from Kansas to eat at Jeannie's, one of whom loves Gooseberry Pie, prompting Jeannie to add it to her arsenal.

About 20 minutes after our conversation ended, my phone rang displaying Shirley's number. When I answered she said only this, "It's not just the Pie that's good, it's the vegetables too."

LEG #1 (2/24/18)

#1 Otoe County - Mary's Cafe (Nebraska City) @ 9:40 AM - $2.98

	Filling	Crust	Visual	Taste	Total	Type
AJ	3	3	3	3	12	Lemon Meringue
Charlie	3	2	2	2	9	Lemon Meringue
Joe	3	3	2	3	11	Chocolate Meringue
					10.67	

#2 Nemaha County - Cafe Metro (Auburn) @ 10:50 AM - $2.95

	Filling	Crust	Visual	Taste	Total	Type
AJ	4	3	3	4	14	Pecan
Charlie	3	2	3	4	12	Caramel Apple
Joe	3	4	3	3	13	Strawberry Rhubarb
					13	

#3 Richardson County - Six Mile Cafe (Dawson) @ 12:20 PM - $2.75

	Filling	Crust	Visual	Taste	Total	Type
AJ	4	5	5	3	17	Gooseberry
Charlie	4	4	3	4	15	Walnut Oatmeal
Joe	5	4	5	5	19	Sour Cream Raisin
					17	

#4 Johnson County - Frazier's Cafe (Tecumseh) @ 1:35 PM - $2.50

	Filling	Crust	Visual	Taste	Total	Type
AJ	3	4	2	5	14	Strawberry Rhubarb
Charlie	2	2	2	2	8	Cherry
Joe	4	3	5	3	15	Apple
					12.33	

#5 Pawnee County - Jeannie's Place (Lewiston) @ 3:15 PM - $0.00   BEST

	Filling	Crust	Visual	Taste	Total	Type
AJ	5	4	5	5	19	Pecan (a la mode)
Charlie	5	5	4	5	19	Strawberry Rhubarb (a la mode)
Joe	5	4	4	5	18	Pecan (a la mode)
					18.67	

It begins...

Pecan at Jeannie's

Six Mile Café

Mary's Café

The almighty Pie board

Café Metro

Jeannie's Place

Feeling good

LEG #2

XANTO!

4/13/18 - 4/14/18 ——————————— **671 Miles**

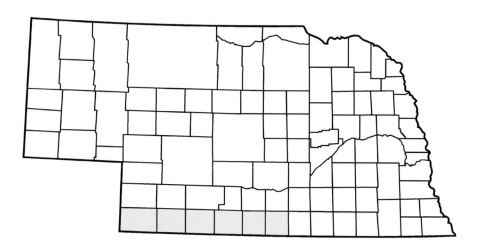

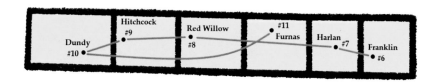

We dug a little deeper on this leg, adding a sixth piece of Pie and staying overnight in Harlan County. All six stops were planned out, but by trip's end we had to audible on three. We had Xanto, the nationwide winter storm to thank for that. Thankfully, we had no issues en route to Franklin County for our first stop in Naponee, the No Where Bar. There we had some very good homemade Pies, made especially for us by the owner's daughter as part of the weekly buffet (which we also enjoyed that Friday night). After our stay in Alma's Western Holiday Motel however, we awoke to brutal winds blowing snow that resulted in what were often whiteout conditions for the early morning.

Our first of five stops on Saturday was KJ's Cafe in Alma, just blocks from our motel. We appeared to be the only car out and about that morning, but KJ's remained open for a successful start. This theme would not continue long. As we entered Furnas County the sky was clearing up and things were looking better, but it was all for naught when we arrived in Cambridge. We encountered the first closed cafe despite our best laid plans, so off to the local grocer we went. Frozen Mrs. Smith's Pies were our only choice, which caused a long debate as we roamed the aisles aimlessly. Do we power through it as is? Or maybe wait for it to thaw and eat it coming back through the county on our way home? Our deliberating caused the manager to inquire about our problem, so we asked her for assistance. Naturally she knew the folks who ran the cafe that closed, immediately calling them for us. She hung up the phone with news that they would open later in the day if the weather continued to cooperate. With that we elected to continue on and let fate decide upon our return.

As we nervously approached McCook in Red Willow County to eat our second piece in three tries, we were relieved to find Sehnert's Bakery up and running, just north of the town's main stretch. As we entered, the first face seen was that of Matt Sehnert's. We know this because he greeted us with these suspicious yet inviting words, "I'm Matt Sehnert, I don't know you guys." There were a lot of amazing looking things in Sehnert's display case that we had to pass on due to fear of a sugar overload so early in the day, but luckily his Pie delivered quite well. Sehnert's was solid across the board, in spite of serving my least favorite kind (Lemon Meringue), which was impressive. This was the point where our plans came off the rails... again.

Our stop in Culbertson also failed us with no hope in sight (at which time we had to push ourselves out of a snow drift), so we blindly continued west, hoping the Pie Gods would smile down on us. As we entered Stratton, a town of 350, we saw Burgers Baskets & More! on the corner of the highway. This was our last chance without a major detour derailing us for the day. Inside we found one Coconut Cream Pie with three slices left! After a nice Pie served up by nice people, we left Hitchcock County with the weather improving each hour. When we reached Haigler, the last town in the southwest corner of the state, we were foiled again by another cafe succumbing to Xanto's powers. The backtracking began with two counties yet to be conquered.

Benkelman, with a population teetering just above 800, was our greatest hope in Dundy County. The legend of Ward Bond, surely watching over us as we entered his boyhood stomping grounds, would have to show us the way. After wandering into some sort of local arcade and furniture shop (together at last!), we were directed to Beth's Bar and Grill at the end of the road. Beth had a different variety for each of us, with freeze dried ice cream to boot, earning us one more check mark on the day's journey. At this point whiteout conditions were back again with the roads often dicey, occasionally decorated with a stranded car well off the shoulder. This stretch found us trying to push a young teenager out of three feet of snow as his dad and posse of friends arrived in two large pickups, much better equipped to help than us. "What were you thinking son?" These were dad's first words to the stranded youngster as we continued on our way, hoping the remainder of our day held more promise than his.

So we crossed back through two counties, only to be denied for a second time by the same cafe in Cambridge, who never did open their doors. On we went to Holbrook, still having no luck after taking another long shot at their local bar, but leaving with a glimmer of hope provided by the only occupant inside. She suggested going to the town of Arapahoe with one seemingly solid possibility. When we found out the restaurant recommended to us had a burst pipe earlier in the day, adding them to the long list of shutdowns, we dejectedly walked into Wagner's Supermarket nearby as a last resort. They had the same frozen Pies we saw in Cambridge... but they also had exactly one boxed Apple Pie in their baked goods section that was ready to eat! After some awkward and funny exchanges about our quest, we were able to convince the owner to cut the Pie for us and let us use the store's breakroom to eat it. When we got upstairs we found a small table and exactly three chairs (and one creepy mannequin). Leg #2 complete.

QUOTES OUT OF CONTEXT

"That man is a liar." - Charlie

"There needs to be a war in that town between the Wagners and everyone else." - AJ

THINGS WE LEARNED

Joe is a liar.

Only with a Cream Pie is entering with a side-fork preferred, possibly even allowable.

Sehnert's Bakery

McCook, Red Willow County

Sehnert's Bakery has been around for generations. Dating back to Matt Sehnert's great great grandparents in Germany and beyond, his family has always been in the baking business. At one time there were seven Sehnert's dotting the Nebraska map, and before Matt's parents moved to McCook in 1957 to open what is now the last remaining location, his grandparents ran their own in Plainview. Matt grew up around the family business, never sure that it was for him. After high school he went to the University of Nebraska-Lincoln, wasting little time traveling the world soon after. When he eventually landed in Denver with his wife Shelly, the pull of his hometown seemed too much to ignore. When they made a pros/cons list in 1990, the scales were tipped and Matt and Shelly took over the bakery. In the 30 years since, they've enjoyed their time in McCook, finding it to be a community with great opportunities for making positive change. Since 2001, Sehnert's has presented a live music series, where their listening room has attracted national acts for their customers to enjoy, like Steve Seskin and Darrell Scott among others.

Sehnert's motto is "Something familiar with a twist." Matt would apply that same sentiment to Red Willow County. The best reason to visit is to be surprised, where newcomers will find a wonderful scene for arts and culture. The community theatre, art guild, orchestra, college and various festivals (Prairie Roots Music, Storytelling and Beer to name only three) are just some of the reasons to make the trip (and maybe even stay). "Making and creating is good for humans" says Matt, which is why he and Shelly have stayed in McCook to raise their three kids, and the reason they do what they do for a living. In all his years running Sehnert's, Matt's favorite moments are when he's able to connect two customers, turning strangers into friends with shared interests that would have otherwise gone unnoticed.

When asked about Sehnert's signature item, Matt couldn't limit it to one. A favorite of his is their Apple Planter Sandwich, which is turkey, bacon, provolone and sliced apple with honey mustard and mayo on focaccia bread. This unique menu item borrows roots from the Sutter Deli in Grand Island where Matt visited many years ago. There's also the loose meat Jiffy Burger, as well as the Bieroc (Sehnert's version winning a 2019 National James Beard award). On the sweeter side of things, Matt took great pride in telling me about the homemade rolls and doughnuts made with locally grown and milled flour from Wauneta Roller Mills, less than an hour away on Hwy 6. One other rarity at the bakery is that their peanut butter rolls outsell their glazed doughnuts, which Matt attributes to McCook being peanut butter crazy... for reasons unknown. This proved true not long after in our conversation when he told me his favorite Pie is Chocolate Peanut Butter. When I noted his regional bias he laughed it off. "I didn't even think about that. It must be me!"

In pondering Sehnert's future, Matt sounded optimistic but uncertain about what exactly it will bring. As he contemplated what will come after the inevitable day he and Shelly hang up their aprons, he finished with this - "If you wanna be a baker, come talk to me."

THE REGULAR:
Tom Wiemers

Tom has been going to Sehnert's as long as he can remember. As a kid, the Saturday morning routine involved an early trip to the bakery for a chocolate sundae before returning home to watch cartoons. Now his family owns a business just down the street, and a few times each week Tom finds his way to Sehnert's for an Apple Chai Tea. His Saturdays have taken a different form since his adolescent days, but they still share a familiar theme. He meets for the Coaches Coffee Club, where the local radio station (96.1 KICX) interviews the area's athletic leaders live inside Sehnert's. The bakery is also stitched into one of the Wiemers' holiday traditions, when Tom picks up his annual Pecan Pie from Sehnert's every Thanksgiving.

LEG #2 (4/13/18 - 4/14/18)

4/13/18 (1 stop)

#6 Franklin County - No Where Bar (Naponee) @ 9:00 PM - $12.99 (w/ Buffet)						BEST

	Filling	Crust	Visual	Taste	Total	Type
AJ	4	3	3	4	14	Chocolate Cream w/ Strawberry Drizzle
Charlie	3	3	3	4	13	Chocolate Cream
Joe	3	4	2	4	13	Coconut Cream
					13.33	

4/14/18 (5 stops)

#7 Harlan County - KJ's Cafe (Alma) @ 7:08 AM - $3.25

	Filling	Crust	Visual	Taste	Total	Type
AJ	3	4	4	1	12	Coconut Cream
Charlie	2	3	3	3	11	Lemon Meringue
Joe	3	3	3	2	11	Reese's Peanut Butter
					11.33	

#8 Red Willow County - Sehnert's Bakery (McCook) @ 9:59 AM - $3.35

	Filling	Crust	Visual	Taste	Total	Type
AJ	4	4	4	4	16	Lemon Meringue
Charlie	3	4	4	4	15	Chocolate Cream
Joe	4	4	4	3	15	Lemon Meringue
					15.33	

#9 Hitchcock County - Burgers Baskets And More! (Stratton) @ 11:25 AM - $3.00 *WC*

	Filling	Crust	Visual	Taste	Total	Type
AJ	4	3	4	4	15	Coconut Cream
Charlie	3	3	4	2	12	Coconut Cream
Joe	3	3	4	3	13	Coconut Cream
					13.33	

#10 Dundy County - Beth's Bar And Grill (Benkelman) @ 12:29 PM (MST) - $2.25 *WC*

	Filling	Crust	Visual	Taste	Total	Type
AJ	3	2	2	2	9	Cherry (a la mode)
Charlie	1	1	3	2	7	Cookies And Cream
Joe	3	3	2	3	11	Peach (a la mode)
					9	

#11 Furnas County - Wagner's Supermarket (Arapahoe) @ 4:15 PM - $2.22 *WC*

	Filling	Crust	Visual	Taste	Total	Type
AJ	2	3	4	3	12	Apple
Charlie	2	2	3	4	11	Apple
Joe	3	3	2	3	11	Apple
					11.33	

Red Willow County

Coconut Cream at Burgers
Baskets and More!

Destiny

Good morning!

Sacred ground

Sehnert's

Still hungry

Stuck

LEG #3

THE GOLD(EN BROWN) STANDARD

5/19/18 ———————————— **311 Miles**

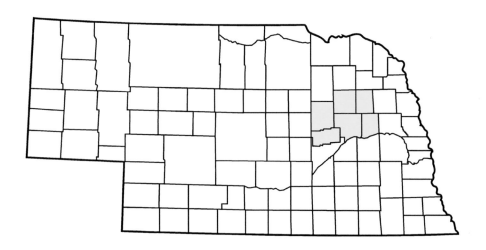

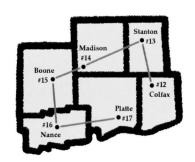

Stanton
#13

Madison
#14

Boone
#15

#12
Colfax

Platte
#17

#16
Nance

A new approach was taken in organizing this leg. Instead of blindly scouring the state via Google Maps until a food icon appeared (yep, that's it, the secret is out), I tried to add a more human element. I decided to reach out to county clerks for their best suggestions, which proved quite effective and entertaining as a starting guide. Three responded with ideas, two were used, the third being a grocery store containing no Pie (still can't figure that one out).

With a solid path ahead, we set out on Saturday morning with high hopes, and Colfax County immediately delivered. As we pulled up to the modest and unassuming storefront of the Clarkson Bakery at the north end of main street, we didn't know what to expect from a place primarily selling kolaches, rolls and bread, and who only made a Pie per special request from us. As we entered and saw five locals drinking coffee at the center table we knew we'd made the right choice. When we asked the woman behind the counter about our Pie, she didn't hesitate before handing us a large box with a note taped to the front describing at length "A group from Lincoln wanting Pie from every county..." The contents within were a mystery to us and the owner alike, whose daughter did the baking. Before the official unveiling, AJ walked to the local market for some plastic cutlery (which sparked the idea of bringing our own personalized forks) since on site Pie eating was not the usual routine for the Clarkson Bakery. When the box was finally opened, our eyes were treated to what was arguably the most beautiful creation known to man. A Rhubarb Pie, and every square millimeter of it perfect. It didn't take long to find out that the taste followed suit. The only two points keeping it from a perfect group rating of 60/60 were AJ and Charlie taking off one point each in the visual category, due to Charlie's lack of serving prowess. This caused quite a stir en route to our next stop, but that's the nature of being a prisoner to your own rules I suppose. After being regaled by the locals with stories of splitting gizzards on the farms where they grew up, and revisiting a family pastime of cutting the heads off of chickens so the kids could cheer them on while the yard got decorated with blood, we decided to let them finish our Pie. Clarkson still had one treasure waiting as we were ushered next door for a beef jerky recommendation. The local butcher there just happened to be related to one of the morning's storytellers.

After such a promising start it was hard to imagine the rest could keep up the momentum. It's true that no other Pie would compete with the magic in Clarkson, but aside from some brief torrential rain the trip unfolded nicely. Our next stop was another deviation from the norm, when someone from Stanton's Veterans of Foreign Wars, Post 3602 agreed to not only make a Pie for us (or a bowl of strawberries as Charlie put it), but to meet and open up shop on a day they'd otherwise be closed. Once again, Nebraska hospitality reigned supreme.

We found more Rhubarb Pie when we met Adam at the City Cafe. He was four years into his dream of running a restaurant after moving from Omaha to Madison County's Newman Grove with his wife and family. Then onto Boone County's Stirred Pot in Albion, where Jacque greeted us and excitedly talked about her son Curtis, the owner and head chef who had opened just weeks earlier and uses only locally sourced ingredients. Nance County gave us our second roadside stop of Pie-braska in Pappy's Place, continuing our smooth run at the junction of Hwy 14 and 22. The final highlight was finding our first Banana Cream Pie at the Picket Fence Cafe in Columbus, a collective desire for the group courtesy of Platte County. There were many options, so only one of us could truly celebrate this victory. Ace of Diamonds. What a glorious finale.

QUOTES OUT OF CONTEXT

"I was thinking of one. Now I'll try to think of one again." - AJ

"It's not Charlie's fault or their fault. It's Charlie's fault." - Joe

THINGS WE LEARNED

The greatness of bacon is still a hotly contested issue.

Charlie can't win.

#12 Colfax County - Clarkson Bakery (Clarkson) @ 9:12 AM - $4.00   BEST

	Filling	Crust	Visual	Taste	Total	Type
AJ	5	5	4	5	19	Rhubarb
Charlie	5	5	4	5	19	Rhubarb
Joe	5	5	5	5	20	Rhubarb
					19.33	

#13 Stanton County - Veterans Of Foreign Wars: Post 3602 (Stanton) @ 10:08 AM - $2.15

	Filling	Crust	Visual	Taste	Total	Type
AJ	3	4	4	5	16	Strawberry (w/ whipped cream)
Charlie	3	4	4	3	14	Strawberry (w/ whipped cream)
Joe	2	4	4	3	13	Strawberry (w/ whipped cream)
					14.33	

#14 Madison County - City Cafe (Newman Grove) @ 11:25 AM - $3.00

	Filling	Crust	Visual	Taste	Total	Type
AJ	4	4	4	3	15	Rhubarb (a la mode)
Charlie	4	5	5	4	18	Double Crust Rhubarb (a la mode)
Joe	4	3	5	3	15	Rhubarb (a la mode)
					16	

#15 Boone County - The Stirred Pot (Albion) @ 12:24 PM - $3.21

	Filling	Crust	Visual	Taste	Total	Type
AJ	3	5	3	4	15	Coconut Cream
Charlie	3	2	3	3	11	Apple (a la mode)
Joe	2	1	3	3	9	Chocolate Meringue
					11.67	

#16 Nance County - Pappy's Place (Fullerton) @ 1:21 PM - $2.59

	Filling	Crust	Visual	Taste	Total	Type
AJ	3	2	3	3	11	Apple
Charlie	2	2	3	2	9	Cherry
Joe	2	3	3	3	11	Pecan
					9.67	

#17 Platte County - Picket Fence Cafe (Columbus) @ 2:45 PM - $3.15

	Filling	Crust	Visual	Taste	Total	Type
AJ	4	5	3	5	17	Sour Cream Raisin
Charlie	4	4	3	4	15	Coconut Cream
Joe	5	5	3	4	17	Banana Cream
					16.33	

Without work there are no kolaches

Adam at City Café

Banana Cream at Picket Fence

Chocolate Meringue at The Stirred Pot

City Café

Nance County

The Holy Grail is in Clarkson!

This way...

LEG #4

A WARM WELCOME

6/16/18 ——————————————— **600 Miles**

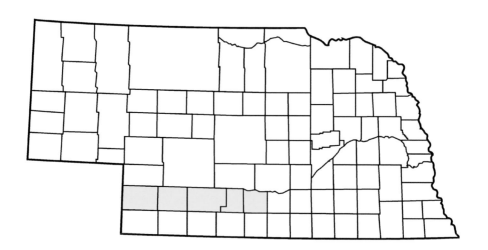

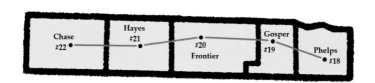

As we returned to southwest Nebraska, scarred by the memories of a disjointed trip served up by Xanto during Leg #2, it was apparent early on this would go very differently. Scorching heat, no overnight stay, and a couple of homemade Pies in off the beaten path locations laid a nice groundwork.

With an early start, we made our first stop at the Cozy Inn Cafe in Holdrege, Phelps County. Before we found the actual entrance, we opened the first door under a labeled awning which led us to someone's back as they washed dishes. Shutting the door quickly and sheepishly, we made our way to the front of the building (what a concept!). After actually entering, we sat down in a booth near the Pie board containing the first Key Lime of Pie-braska. This eventually led to an early argument about what color the inside of a lime was. This was prompted by Charlie and I finding it strange that the Pie served to AJ (Ace of Clubs) was white without a hint of green. After some research, we were both kiiiind of correct, but the waitress sided with AJ (who I hate to admit was actually correct). She was also sure we weren't from Holdrege, so we asked what gave it away. "I know lots of people" was her response, channeling her inner Matt Sehnert. It turned out she was right. Solid cafe. Good Pie options. Great start.

Gosper County offered the best landscapes thus far as we drove into and out of Elwood for our second stop, however the Pies left something to be desired. Our hunch was that we were served warmed up Pie from the Village PieMaker (a known Pie company in Nebraska that ships frozen to locations all over the place, founded out of Eustis in Frontier County), which wasn't confirmed at the time but would soon be debunked (see Leg #5). Because of this known institution in the neighboring county, the folks at B's Cafe expected us to make that our next stop. Naturally, this wasn't the case since we were out to experience all things unknown and new, so instead we opted for the Curtis Cattle Company, a choice made with zero regret. This was a large, open space lacking activity when we arrived, with the waitress immediately dubbing us the "Pie Guys." We decided to eat a meal there along with our usual, which proved well worth it, as the CCC served up extremely generous portions. Of course we had our Pie first so as not to disturb our shaky, unrefined palates. With my back to the bar, I saw Charlie's eyes widen and his mouth literally drop open. Seconds later we were each presented with the biggest piece of Pie we'd yet seen (served in a bowl with a spoon). They were delicious too, and we found out were made by the waitress's mother-in-law, who has yet to release the recipe to another living soul, and whose cinnamon rolls sell for $250 to the locals during charity drives. We could see why. This turned out to be the highest rated Pie of the trip by a wide margin, earning the second 20-point rating of Pie-braska from AJ. However, the best story of the day was still ahead of us.

The McKillip Guest House at the south end of Hayes Center was where we were sent by Sue Messersmith, the County Clerk for Hayes. Not knowing what to expect, we drove up to the lavish house of Pie and found a small audience waiting. After Cindy, the owner of the house, greeted and welcomed us inside, we were met not only by Sue (who was one of the Pie makers) but also the county's Economic Developer and a representative from the local paper. There was great enthusiasm from everyone, and like all others we'd met, they were a bit perplexed as to why we were doing this. Of course, no suitable answers were given. After we were heavily recruited to establish residence in Hayes County (specifically AJ for his electrical skills), we were told about their County Fair. This is a week-long event at the end of July which includes one of, if not the biggest, livestock shows in the state. Do you know what else they have a large amount of entries for in an annual contest? You guessed it... Pie. After being formally asked to judge, we knew this was no opportunity to pass up and immediately accepted.

At the end of this wonderful stop we were given directions to Imperial in Chase County. We took gravel roads to get into Hayes Center, and would do the same going out. It was nice in the smartphone era to get verbal directions about where to turn and how far to go based on landmarks like "well kept cemeteries." Our 22nd stop of Pie-braska would be another to warm the heart, as we were helped by our second consecutive Cindy, who after striking out with all possible stops, offered to bake us a Pie herself from the comfort of her home. We arrived and found Cindy and her husband Jeff outside to greet us, and were promptly invited to take a seat at their kitchen table. She baked us a mini Cherry Pie and sent us home with the leftovers. And with that our fourth outing came to a close, but not without another 20-pointer and our first invite to judge a Pie contest. We would be seeing Hayes County again very soon.

QUOTES OUT OF CONTEXT

"I had a bag of Skittles." - Charlie

"I'm not a Pie server! I'm a Pie eater!" - AJ

THINGS WE LEARNED

Charlie doesn't know how to fill up a gas tank.

Rainbows are a regular occurrence... or are they?

LEG #4 (6/16/18)

#18 Phelps County - Cozy Inn Cafe (Holdrege) @ 9:34 AM - $3.75

	Filling	Crust	Visual	Taste	Total	Type
AJ	4	4	2	4	14	Key Lime
Charlie	2	3	4	4	13	Banana Cream
Joe	4	4	4	3	15	Turtle
					14	

#19 Gosper County - B's Cafe (Elwood) @ 10:42 AM - $2.00

	Filling	Crust	Visual	Taste	Total	Type
AJ	3	2	2	1	8	Peach
Charlie	4	3	3	4	14	Peach
Joe	3	2	2	2	9	Apple
					10.33	

#20 Frontier County - Curtis Cattle Company (Curtis) @ 11:55 AM - $4.00

	Filling	Crust	Visual	Taste	Total	Type
AJ	5	5	5	5	20	Chocolate Cream
Charlie	5	4	3	5	17	Chocolate Cream
Joe	5	5	5	4	19	Coconut Cream
					18.67	

#21 Hayes County - The McKillip Guest House (Hayes Center) @ 1:45 PM - $0.00 `BEST`

	Filling	Crust	Visual	Taste	Total	Type
AJ	4	3	3	4	14	Peanut Butter
Charlie	3	4	3	3	13	White Chocolate
Joe	3	4	2	3	12	White Chocolate
					13	

#22 Chase County - Local Residence (Imperial) @ 2:45 PM (MST) - $0.00

	Filling	Crust	Visual	Taste	Total	Type
AJ	4	3	2	3	12	Cherry
Charlie	4	3	2	3	12	Cherry
Joe	4	3	3	3	13	Cherry
					12.33	

Approaching the McKillip House of Pie

Coconut Cream at Curtis Cattle

Cozy Inn Café

Curtis Cattle Company

Phelps County

Runnin' with the Pack

Sue and Cindy at the McKillip

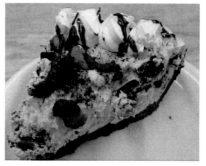

Turtle at Cozy Inn Café

COUNTY FAIR CONTESTS

THE PIE GUYS HAVE ARRIVED

7/31/18 & 8/9/18

---

648 Miles

A brief interlude from checking counties off our list had us judging two County Fair Pie contests. Not only did we head back to Hayes Center, but it also happened that our local paper in Lincoln put a story out that same day on the "Pie Guys." This caused enough of a stir for Cass County to ask us to oversee their Fair as well, but more on that later.

We returned for a stay at the McKillip Guest House in Hayes Center to gear up for our public debut (we drew cards to see who got the master suite with the private bath... Ace of Diamonds). As we walked across town the following morning to take in a bit of the horse show, we were called out by more than one resident as the Pie Guys. Was this because we each decided to wear cheaply personalized shirts showcasing that very moniker, or was our newfound celebrity starting to catch up with us? I'd like to believe the latter.

The folks putting it on were excited to see us, and we were excited to see an impressive array of 47 Pies. It was a very laid back affair, and we were given all the time we wanted to assess the ins and outs of each entry. We didn't stray far from our usual system, but changed our format slightly to make more sense of this somewhat overwhelming process. We let each other be for the most part, allowing ourselves to mull over what worked and what didn't without being swayed. Controversy still managed to creep in after AJ and I were presented with what we thought to be the best Pecan Pie possible. Charlie was given the exact same Pie but strongly disagreed, and the raucous that ensued very likely concerned at least a couple Hayes residents.

In the end it all worked out, and we had a unanimous winner with a superb Sour Cream Raisin. We were invited back to judge in 2019 (possibly because the winner happened to be the organizer as well), and we happily accepted. They even tried to pay us! As if staying for free in one of the nicest homes in the state, being given 47 free pieces of Pie and topping it off with a hamburger wasn't enough.

Hardly a week went by before we did the same in Cass County. While our day in Hayes was great, it was extremely low-key and somewhere near our expectations in setting, and I mean that in the best possible way. In Cass County however, we drove up to hundreds of cars and thousands of people. Ferris wheels, carnival games, country bands and livestock. You name it, they had it. If you've seen a Fair in a movie or on TV, this was it. We found the Pie spot with some luck, and saw that our article from the Lincoln Journal Star was posted on the front door of their Expo Center. We didn't know what we had gotten into.

Upon entering, we found three chairs placed at the front of the room, where an audience was already waiting excitedly, presumably for our arrival! I overheard a woman talking to a friend about the event, exclaiming that her daughters were "so excited when they heard the Pie Guys were coming." What was happening?! We were later told that Pie entries doubled after hearing of our planned appearance. To further the insanity, we were introduced to a couple of experts who were judging the Pumpkin Pie entries exclusively, and we were chosen to cover all other fields. This was the moment that really emphasized how absurd and awesome this was. The Pie judging veteran of 20+ years told us about his credentials and his methods of assessment. We nodded, pretending to relate.

Taking our seats, the three of us were given 23 full Pies to cut, eat and rate. All in front of a very attentive audience waiting for commentary as we went through our slices. We filled the gap on our provided microphone as best we could, but along the way kept it lighthearted and explained that our "process" was a bit more laid back and more of a gut reaction to say the least. Everyone had fun with it, not least of all us. The top three were all fruit, including a Saskatoon Berry (a new one for each of us), but an immaculate Blueberry took home the crown. We were invited back for 2019 in Cass County also, putting us well on our way to becoming a revered institution throughout the state.

The Cass County marquee

Hayes County's finest

Cass County looks on

Hard at work in Hayes

The secret of life revealed in Cass County

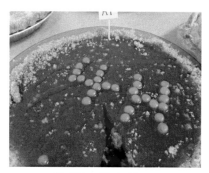

Red Hots Pie in Hayes

Hayes County, laid to waste

Three winners... and three other guys

LEG #5

OUT OF THE "ORD"INARY

9/8/18 ——————————— **411 Miles**

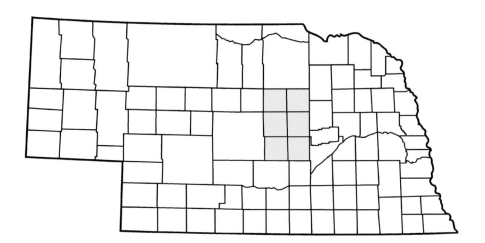

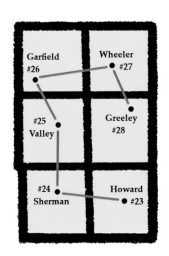

After a three month hiatus from Pie-braska to take our undeserved seats at the judging tables for Hayes and Cass County, we were back on the road. This leg felt a bit thrown together after finding some early difficulty in nailing down our stops, but in the end turned out to be a great run.

At our first stop in Howard County we met Alice, who ran the Sweet Shoppe in St. Paul. And hers is no typical diner, but one adorned by hundreds of cookie jars in all shapes, sizes and characters. Every inch of wall space was covered, instantly ranking the Sweet Shoppe high on our list of best environments to have an early morning slice. Charlie won a rare first pick to start the day and scored the coveted Sour Cream Raisin we all wanted. After Alice graciously said all the Pies were on the house, we asked her mother who was conveniently sitting at the table nearest the register to take our photo. Alice quickly stopped us and grabbed another waitress for camera duty, saying that her mother is notorious for "cutting off heads" in photos (her mother concurred). The breakfasts looked great too, but we couldn't fill up on stop #1, so we'll have to come back again. Excellent start.

Sherman County brought another nice stop at the Loup City Diner, where some Pie was prepared on our behalf. Just another benefit of being the Pie Guys I guess. After leaving and heading to North Loup, we realized that virtually every sign since Lincoln showed the distance to Ord, no matter where we were or where we were heading. The Pie Gods must have been trying to tell us something about Ord that was yet unknown, but we soldiered on into Valley County as scheduled. We arrived at our undisclosed destination, walked in, were shown to a table, and then heard the words that nightmares are made of. "We're out of Pie." This was particularly puzzling since we had this stop's Pie confirmed, but we quickly went into audible mode and asked the waitress for recommendations nearby (an awkward situation, but it wouldn't be our last like it). She gave us a few, all of which were in... yep, Ord. This took us a bit out of route but it had to be done. We struck out with all the given options, even checking out every food truck that was setting up in the town square for their annual Scratchtoberfest (look it up). No luck. Heading north out of town we stumbled into Speeds' Apple Market just before we hit the edge. We had to go with a full Pie, but scored our first Pumpkin in the process (sure, it was a Tippin's, but it was Pumpkin). The deli clerk was extremely kind and helpful, cutting the Pie for us and sitting down to chat while we talked about our travels. A Kentucky native, she recommended we go there for some "Derby

Pie." Someday nice deli lady, someday.

Garfield County brought Verda's Cafe in Burwell and Apple Pie for all. Nothing against Verda's, but Apple was becoming the consensus least favorite of the group. America's favorite just didn't happen to be ours I guess, and this is where it started to become a bit of a thing. Barlett in Wheeler County brought what was voted the best stop of the day in the Bibs and Boots Cafe. We met Dorothy Dexter and her daughter who ran the place, which we had all to ourselves (likely due to the opening game of the season for Husker football and the Scott Frost era). They were very enthusiastic about having us in their Cafe, telling us all about their business, family, town Bronze Garden (we gave ourselves a tour), and asking about our adventures as well. When Charlie mentioned the now famed Rhubarb Pie from Clarkson, Dorothy quickly exited the dining area and went to the kitchen, only to return with a tupperware of homemade rhubarb jam that she demanded Charlie take home free of charge. They gave us some great Pie, and bullied us into (not that we needed it) ordering their signature burger with the thickest bacon on earth. It turned out to be one of the best decisions we (they) ever made.

The day ended with yet another great grocery store stop at Esch's in Spalding, Greeley County. The store owners were kind enough to take our call earlier in the day and coordinate taking home a frozen Pie, baking it for us, and returning it to the store ready to eat. It was a Peach Pie courtesy of the Village PieMaker (sound familiar?). This confirmed without a doubt we had yet to try one, contrary to previous opinion. Knowing that they're frozen Pies shipped all over the region, our expectations were admittedly low, but we were extremely impressed and happy to have our first taste on an official Pie-braska leg. It helped that we were directed to eat it on top of the town dam and fish ladder (we didn't know what that meant either). So there we were, eating our warm Peach Pie on a picnic table atop the fish ladder grating feeding back into the local lake. Another great day, and one that turned out to be much more fruitful for us than the Huskers.

QUOTES OUT OF CONTEXT

"Peach is like the Apple of Peach." - AJ

"What county are we in?" - Joe;
(Looks at his watch in silence... not joking) - Charlie

"How can I rate this Pie?" - Charlie;
"Like all the rest!" - AJ

THINGS WE LEARNED

Bacon is great again.

Charlie and watches don't mix.

SPOTLIGHT:
Sweet Shoppe
St. Paul, Howard County

The Sweet Shoppe's roots were modest, starting in a 12 x 22 foot space with four tables and a maximum capacity of twelve. This is where Alice Osterman and her mother began selling ice cream, cookies and Pies to the locals of St. Paul. After two years they moved across the street and upped the occupancy to forty, where they spent the next four years. In 1993, Alice and mom made it to their current location, which was previously occupied for decades by the Bartles Dry Goods Store, and started serving up to 200 people.

Alice's journey to the Sweet Shoppe was anything but typical. Before coming to St. Paul, where her mom called home, Alice spent a year traveling. Her direction was guided by the mantra "anything but banking," which she left Alaska to get away from. Mom was working at a local nursing home in St. Paul where Alice jumped on board. When the owner asked if she had ever cooked and her reply was "only for my family," he said that'll be just fine. This was her earliest foray into preparing food for the masses, and she grew to love it. She also grew to love the town of St. Paul and the surrounding region, where good people weren't hard to find, and they were proud of their history. None more specifically than the Museum of Nebraska Major League Baseball just a few doors down from the Sweet Shoppe on Howard Ave, where local legend Grover Cleveland Alexander is heavily featured.

When I asked Alice what the Sweet Shoppe is most known for, there are two very notable draws. Aside from many Pie options, including two of Alice's personal favorites, Sour Cream Raisin and Coconut Cream, the Shoppe features fried chicken on Wednesdays (a tradition dating back to the days of their four table setup). I'm told the locals count the days of the week by saying Monday, Tuesday, Chicken Day, Thursday... And then there are the cookie jars. 1,802 of them to be exact (an ever growing number, the grand total likely being higher as you read this). It started early when the first jar Alice purchased was a teddy bear with overalls to place in the window. Not long after, she found a companion teddy and the flood gates opened. The initial criteria was simply that if a jar reminded her of the Sweet Shoppe, she would add it to the collection, saying that if it made her smile she was sure it would do the same for someone else. Eventually, they arrived in droves by gift or donation. When I asked her to name her favorite of the whole lot, she didn't hesitate long before citing her Emmett Kelly Coca-Cola machine. It's an original and the very last of its kind, and a likeness of someone Alice has always admired for bringing joy and inspiration to so many people throughout the years. Something she's become rather familiar with herself.

THE REGULARS:
Roger, Lee, Jim & Lonnie

Every Tuesday morning, "The Fellas" like to convene at the Sweet Shoppe to solve all the world's problems. For over ten years this has been their spot, and they keep coming back as Roger said, because "Alice treats us fair and pretends she likes us." Referring to themselves as the Breakfast Club, there was a definite feeling of comfortable camaraderie as we chatted. Roger even said there's a direct connection for the group and the cookie jar decorum, as his wife has donated more than a few. "She also makes each of us dust 14 of 'em before we can get fed," he playfully added. And when they do get fed, they order with their own off-menu lingo that's well known to Alice and others. Lonnie will order the "Harley Davidson 370," Jim the "211 S," and it rarely fails that someone will get a "Doo da day with ham," the Sweet Shoppe's famous breakfast sandwich. There are no plans to stop the Breakfast Club ritual, because where there's good food and good friends, gatherings will follow. Right around this time our phone conversation came to an abrupt end when Roger suddenly and nicely interjected, saying "Well my breakfast is here, so you know what that does to you!" Yes sir, I do. Enjoy.

LEG #5 (9/8/18)

#23 Howard County - Sweet Shoppe (St. Paul) @ 9:05 AM - $0.00

	Filling	Crust	Visual	Taste	Total	Type
AJ	4	3	2	3	12	Coconut Cream
Charlie	3	4	3	3	13	Sour Cream Raisin
Joe	3	2	2	3	10	Strawberry Rhubarb
					11.67	

#24 Sherman County - Loup City Diner (Loup City) @ 10:25 AM - $4.00

	Filling	Crust	Visual	Taste	Total	Type
AJ	3	4	3	3	13	Cherry
Charlie	4	3	2	5	14	Pecan
Joe	5	3	3	5	16	Pecan
					14.33	

#25 Valley County - Speeds' Apple Market (Ord) @ 12:38 AM - $3.00 *WC*

	Filling	Crust	Visual	Taste	Total	Type
AJ	4	4	3	3	14	Pumpkin
Charlie	3	3	1	3	10	Pumpkin
Joe	4	3	3	3	13	Pumpkin
					12.33	

#26 Garfield County - Verda's Cafe (Burwell) @ 1:08 PM - $2.00

	Filling	Crust	Visual	Taste	Total	Type
AJ	4	4	3	4	15	Apple
Charlie	2	3	3	2	10	Apple
Joe	4	4	3	3	14	Apple
					13	

#27 Wheeler County - Bibs & Boots Cafe (Bartlett) @ 2:15 PM - $2.65 `BEST`

	Filling	Crust	Visual	Taste	Total	Type
AJ	5	5	4	3	17	Peach
Charlie	4	4	4	4	16	Peach
Joe	5	5	5	3	18	Coconut Cream
					17	

#28 Greeley County - Esch's Grocery (Spalding) @ 4:20 PM - $4.00 *WC*

	Filling	Crust	Visual	Taste	Total	Type
AJ	4	5	2	5	16	Peach
Charlie	4	4	3	4	15	Peach
Joe	4	5	4	4	17	Peach
					16	

Alice puts her stamp on Pie-braska

Charlie and Dorothy at Bibs and Boots

Charlie on the fish ladder

Coconut Meringue at Bibs and Boots

Getting bronzed in Bartlett

Inside the Sweet Shoppe

Valley County

We did

LEG #6

SHAMROCKS &
DESIGNER SOCKS

11/16/18 - 11/17/18 ———————————— 642 Miles

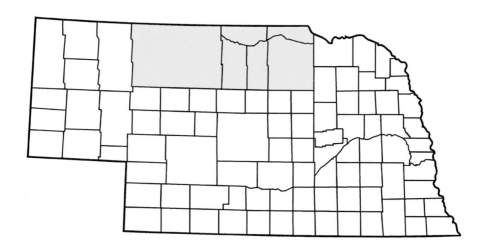

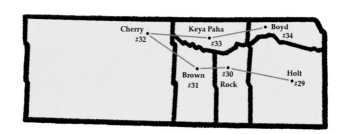

North Central Nebraska called for another overnighter to fit in a full day of Pie on a cold November Saturday. The Westside Restaurant in Holt County's city of O'Neill provided our first slice in some time right before our dinner (just like Mom always wanted), then we were off to the Historic Golden Hotel just down the road. Perched on the northeast corner of the main intersection in town, we needed only to look out of our room's window to get a good view of the world's largest shamrock painted in the street. The stay was nice, despite multiple employees being strangely concerned that one of us planned to sleep on their floor. We never understood this point of emphasis that came up more than twice, but if anyone from the Hotel is reading this (what an absurd idea) you can rest assured we all remained elevated above ground level for the duration. We did however stack up multiple chairs and various items against the bathroom door more than once, in hopes of an avalanche when opened by a Pie Guy... after all, we weren't told not to.

We began the next morning with Bassett's Lodge & Range Cafe in Rock County. Daunitta at the County Clerk's office helped with this one, saying that only during hunting season do they serve Pie, and they were ready for us with camera in hand. This led to another local newspaper printing a bit of our story, which continues to astonish, but is always appreciated.

This leg had a good variety of stops, with many settings represented from family restaurant to bar to cafe to converted house. All were modest and quickly accommodating, giving us the smoothest trip so far as we moved just over a third of the way through our county list. During our last stop at the Naper Cafe of Boyd County, we even managed to find Charlie a sock soulmate in our server, Amber. Good luck getting your boys into eccentric socks Amber... they can't all be like Charlie!

We passed the 3,000-mile mark on this one and ended it with a nearly five-hour drive home following our last piece, which Charlie and I tried to power through by playing a movie guessing game (AJ went headlong into his favorite pastime of sleeping). This helped distract us through what turned out to be bad winter conditions as we neared home, but also managed to uncover my shameful non-viewings of Bill & Ted's Excellent Adventure and The Muppet Movie. It looks like I have some work to do before our next trip.

QUOTES OUT OF CONTEXT

"Tasted like cough syrup." - AJ

"Did you do a goop test?" - AJ

THINGS WE LEARNED

Hunters have a real sweet tooth.

Jumanji is an American movie classic.

LEG #6 (11/16/18 - 11/11/18)

11/16/18 (1 stop)

#29 Holt County - Westside Restaurant (O'Neill) @ 7:40 PM - $3.89

	Filling	Crust	Visual	Taste	Total	Type
AJ	2	3	2	1	8	Strawberry Rhubarb
Charlie	2	3	3	3	11	Pecan
Joe	4	3	3	4	14	Peach
					11	

11/17/18 (5 stops)

#30 Rock County - Bassett Lodge & Range Cafe (Bassett) @ 8:49 AM - $1.50   **BEST**

	Filling	Crust	Visual	Taste	Total	Type
AJ	4	3	3	4	14	Strawberry Rhubarb
Charlie	3	3	4	4	14	Strawberry Rhubarb
Joe	4	3	4	3	14	Strawberry Rhubarb
					14	

#31 Brown County - D & B Cafe (Ainsworth) @ 9:40 AM - $2.25

	Filling	Crust	Visual	Taste	Total	Type
AJ	3	4	2	3	12	Cherry
Charlie	4	3	4	3	14	Apple
Joe	3	4	3	2	12	Peach
					12.67	

#32 Cherry County - Coachlight Cafe (Valentine) @ 10:54 AM - $4.00

	Filling	Crust	Visual	Taste	Total	Type
AJ	4	4	4	4	16	Coconut Cream
Charlie	4	4	2	4	14	Lemon Meringue
Joe	4	3	5	4	16	Sour Cream Raisin
					15.33	

#33 Keya Paha County - Cattleman's Lounge (Springview) @ 12:20 PM - $2.75

	Filling	Crust	Visual	Taste	Total	Type
AJ	2	4	4	4	14	Sour Cream Raisin
Charlie	4	4	4	4	16	Butterscotch
Joe	3	4	4	5	16	Banana Cream
					15.33	

#34 Boyd County - Naper Cafe (Naper) @ 1:37 PM - $3.00

	Filling	Crust	Visual	Taste	Total	Type
AJ	3	3	4	3	13	Pumpkin (w/ whipped cream)
Charlie	3	1	2	2	8	Cherry
Joe	4	3	4	4	15	Pumpkin (w/ whipped cream)
					12	

"...and I haven't seen a rainbow since!"

Cattleman's Lounge

Charlie and Amber at Naper Café

D & B Café

Sour Cream Raisin at Coachlight Café

Boyd County

Zebra House of Rock County

LEG #7

SIRLOIN A LA MODE

1/26/19 ——————————— **187 Miles**

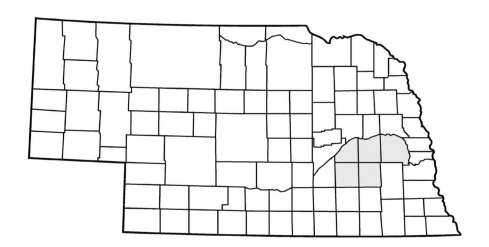

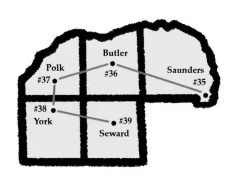

Given our history of trekking for Pie almost exclusively during treacherous weather, planning a January road trip in Nebraska was tempting fate. In preparation, we made this our shortest leg. My concern and worry turned out to be for nothing, and the shovel thrown in the trunk to battle the snow ended up being used as nothing more than the impetus for many jokes about burying each other.

Cheri O's of Saunders County was very inviting on Ashland's vibrant main street. It was more bustling than most, yet presented a recurring problem we'd run into before. We were asked if we wanted our Pie served with ice cream. At any other time in life this would be a welcome addition, but when you're judging Pie, should ice cream be a factor? Will it affect the integrity of the Pie? Make the crust soggy? Skew the look? You can see the bind we sometimes find ourselves in. Given the nature of it all and our eagerness to take in what any diner or cafe has to offer, our response was and always had been up to that point "We'll take it however you normally serve it." Whether they "normally" serve it with ice cream or not probably takes a backseat to us giving the green light to charge an extra $1.50 each. So I got hot Cherry Pie with a quickly melting scoop of vanilla on top. In theory I think we made the right choice, but in practice the ratings felt the sting of this combination.

We were hardly given time to catch our breath before being met with the same challenge in Butler County at the Northside Cafe of David City. This time the Pie came *on* a bed of soft serve ice cream and was served in a bowl. We once again took it as it came, but admittedly were a bit more intrigued than usual due to their method. In the end it didn't add any bonus to how we rated the Pie, but it did allow me to drink the end of my Pie the way I finish my cereal... so that was new.

Stromsburg's Corner Cafe upped the ante and baked three Pies when they heard we were coming. I'm so glad I'm a Pie Guy. I can attest that the Chocolate was near flawless. Everything about the Corner Cafe was impressive, including Jessica and Connie, who served and made our food respectively (including my first ever pizza burger!). We not only enjoyed our time spent in the "Cougar Corner" of Polk County, but also got a recommendation for Hamilton County on a future leg. Eight miles down the road and just barely into York County we got more impressive Pie from PK's, including the oft elusive Rhubarb (and a nudge to make our way to the Purple Pie Place in South Dakota... we'll stow that idea away for the next book). It was double crust, unlike the still remaining standard bearer in Clarkson, but was stellar nonetheless. Most importantly, it was in the town of Benedict where we discovered how weak our reading skills were. Stranger still, it was the word "sirloin" that appeared to be ghost-written throughout the heartland. Earlier in the day a sign outside of someone's home/junk-yard had read "No dumpin' stealin' or lookin.'" AJ's response was wondering why a residence had to advertise it had "No dumpling or sirloin steak." He was ridiculed accordingly. Then we pulled into Benedict, and just blocks before our stop we crossed "Shiloh St." This caused me to scream "SIRLOIN ST!" with the most excitement I could muster. I don't have to tell you how that was received by my carmates, but I guess I'll chalk it up to the power of suggestion.

Goehner in Seward County gave us Chez Bubba, which ended the trip nicely with solid Pies all around in the recently opened venue. It was great to have just a 30-minute trip home upon completion, even if it involved another house with a puzzling sign. This one read "A Dream Died Here." I'm not a superstitious man, but it made me eager to get our eighth leg underway before that prophecy rang true.

QUOTES OUT OF CONTEXT

"When did we start talking about Brazil nuts?" - AJ;
"It's happening now." - Joe

"I was wrong, but you were wrong too! Now I need a
shovel." - Joe

THINGS WE LEARNED

AJ is not the city planner of Ashland.

South Dakota is a state.

LEG #7 (1/26/19)

#35 Saunders County - Cheri O's (Ashland) @ 8:50 AM - $5.00

	Filling	Crust	Visual	Taste	Total	Type
AJ	4	1	3	3	11	Dutch Apple (a la mode)
Charlie	3	1	4	3	11	Dutch Apple (a la mode)
Joe	3	2	3	3	11	Cherry (a la mode)
					11	

#36 Butler County - Northside Cafe (David City) @ 10:40 AM - $2.49

	Filling	Crust	Visual	Taste	Total	Type
AJ	2	3	1	2	8	Apple Nut (a la mode)
Charlie	3	2	1	3	9	Apple Nut (a la mode)
Joe	4	3	2	3	12	Apple Nut (a la mode)
					9.67	

#37 Polk County - Corner Cafe (Stromsburg) @ 11:58 AM - $2.25 `BEST`

	Filling	Crust	Visual	Taste	Total	Type
AJ	5	4	4	5	18	Coconut Cream
Charlie	4	4	3	2	13	Lemon Meringue
Joe	5	5	5	4	19	Chocolate Cream
					16.67	

#38 York County - PK's (Benedict) @ 1:00 PM - $2.75

	Filling	Crust	Visual	Taste	Total	Type
AJ	4	5	3	5	17	Peanut Butter Banana
Charlie	4	5	4	4	17	Peach
Joe	5	4	4	5	18	Rhubarb
					17.33	

#39 Seward County - Chez Bubba (Goehner) @ 1:58 PM - $3.50

	Filling	Crust	Visual	Taste	Total	Type
AJ	4	4	4	5	17	Pecan
Charlie	4	4	5	4	17	Chocolate Pecan
Joe	5	3	5	3	16	Reese's
					16.67	

Butler County

Cheri O's

Corner Café

In the Cougar Corner

Chocolate Cream at Corner Café

Apple Nut at Northside Café

Cut us a slice Mike

Plan B when you're out of wiper fluid

LEG #8

DUDE, WHERE'S MY PIE?

3/2/19 ——————————— **342 Miles**

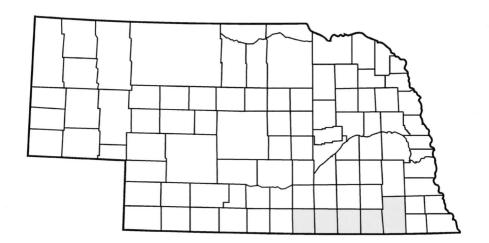

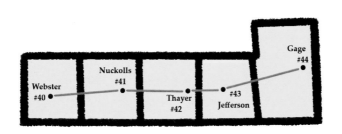

Our dream didn't die in Goehner, but impending death was once again felt on this eighth run. We picked another day plagued by the polar vortex, which was sweeping through the entire Midwest. None of this changed that the Moonstone Bookstore in Red Cloud was poised for our arrival. With a shortage of eateries available in Webster County, Red Cloud local Bob Beardslee answered the call to make sure we would not go hungry. Entering the town's house of books, we found two tables already set with ten pieces of Cinnamon Apple Pie. Our generous Pie baker was joined by local author and store proprietor, Peter Osborne, as well as folks from the local paper, the town historian, an impressive brewer of cider and a few more regulars. Bob shared with me the editorial he had already written for the Red Cloud readers, and we were interviewed for another article as well. However, we couldn't let this rush of fame go to our heads and forget the reason we came, as Bob's old family staple rose above what we'd come to expect from an Apple Pie. The hardest part was trying to concentrate on rating our Pies amidst all the hubbub, which was a welcome change, but a change nonetheless. It's hard to beat a start that offers what Moonstone did, and we were given several suggestions of where to stop on our route back east on Hwy 136 (not least of which was the world's largest porch swing in Hebron, NE).

Next up was Nuckolls County, Pie courtesy of Ruskin. With a population hovering around 100, Ruskin doesn't boast a very long main drag, but it had at least two things going for it that were quickly evident. A stone park bench with "Jim" etched on it in large lettering, and a diner owner dedicated to a nice variety of Pie. Sandra seemed relieved and a bit surprised when we walked into the Broken Spoke, a restaurant she opened just over 20 years ago (I have the koozies to prove it). We were the only activity on a day when weather scared others away, but still saw four untouched Pies sitting on her kitchen counter. Sandra laughed telling us she stayed up until 11:00 the night before to get them ready, then said "I was sure this was a hoax. Who does something like this?" We do, Sandra. We do. She made a mean Coconut Cream, one of the best I've had, and the Spoke's menu also gave me the opportunity to have my second ever pizza burger. I didn't pass it up.

Things were going so well that the good folks of Thayer and Jefferson County decided they would throw some wrenches in our plans. Both counties had cafes who confirmed they'd have Pie well in advance of this trip, but alas, it was not meant to be. The Pioneers Inn of Gilead saved the day for Thayer, with just a few miles of road left before we would hit Jefferson County. When we got to our original Jefferson stop we were told that a Pie was made specifically for us, but a women's bridge club with more than one sweet tooth dropped by earlier in the day, and they decided to sell it all. Aggravating? Sure. But thanks to the help of an old friend and recent Fairbury local, we were escorted to Ray's Apple Market where there were many choices of Pie by the slice in their bakery. We had a good time relaxing in the back of the grocery store as Deb and Jeanie laughed quizzically at us from behind the deli counter. Deb was sure we were up to no good... she may have been right.

Our last stop in Virginia boasted the smallest population we'd yet seen (67), which you'd never guess by walking into Terry's Steakhouse on a Saturday night in Gage County. The place was packed, likely due to their prime rib special, which we each had for dessert to follow our main course of Pie. After all that sugar and a pizza burger each, Charlie and I found the prime rib to be pretty taxing on our insides, but very much worth it. Per the rules, AJ had the exclusive honor of judging our very first crust made entirely of Rice Krispies. Terry's wife Pam was kind enough to send us each home with an additional piece on the house so Charlie and I wouldn't be left wondering after the votes were tallied. Sadly, the ratings from two of us will forever remain a mystery, never to be transcribed to the written page as an official document. Off the record, I thought it was pretty good.

QUOTES OUT OF CONTEXT

"Can you help me with something?" - Old Man shoveling snow;
"Sure." - Charlie;
"Let me know when we're having fun." - Old Man

"Make a Foote note." - Charlie

THINGS WE LEARNED

Trust nobody.

Willa Cather didn't spend as much time in Nebraska as I was led
to believe.

LEG #8 (3/2/19)

#40 Webster County - Moonstone Bookstore (Red Cloud) @ 10:20 AM - $6.66

	Filling	Crust	Visual	Taste	Total	Type
AJ	4	4	4	4	16	Cinnamon Apple (a la mode)
Charlie	3	5	4	3	15	Cinnamon Apple (a la mode)
Joe	3	4	4	3	14	Cinnamon Apple (a la mode)
					15	

#41 Nuckolls County - Broken Spoke (Ruskin) @ 11:45 AM - $2.00

	Filling	Crust	Visual	Taste	Total	Type
AJ	2	3	3	3	11	Cherry
Charlie	3	3	3	3	12	Sour Cream Raisin
Joe	5	5	4	5	19	Coconut Cream
					14	

#42 Thayer County - Pioneers Inn (Gilead) @ 1:58 PM - $1.50 *WC*

	Filling	Crust	Visual	Taste	Total	Type
AJ	5	2	4	4	15	Coconut Cream
Charlie	4	3	3	5	15	Peach
Joe	3	3	2	4	12	Pecan
					14	

#43 Jefferson County - Ray's Apple Market (Fairbury) @ 3:00 PM - $1.99 *WC*

	Filling	Crust	Visual	Taste	Total	Type
AJ	2	3	1	2	8	Strawberry Rhubarb
Charlie	2	3	2	3	10	Apple
Joe	4	3	4	3	14	Peanut Butter
					10.67	

#44 Gage County - Terry's Steakhouse (Virginia) @ 6:00 PM - $3.25   BEST

	Filling	Crust	Visual	Taste	Total	Type
AJ	4	4	3	5	16	Peanut Butter
Charlie	2	3	2	2	9	Coconut Cream
Joe	3	3	3	3	12	Coconut Cream
					12.33	

Thayer County

Broken Spoke

Chatting with the locals of Red Cloud

Deb & Jeanie at Ray's

Sandra at the Broken Spoke

Cinnamon Apple at Moonstone

World's Largest Porch Swing

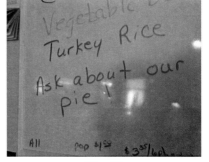

We will!

Ninety-Three Counties, Countless Bites of Pie

Hayes Center, Nebraska - Ten years ago, three college roomates came up with a crazy idea to take a road trip around Nebraska. The idea was not centered around Nebraska scenery, but to taste pie in every county of Nebraska. Yes, you read that right, taste a slice of pie in every county! As many of us can relate, life got in the way of their crazy idea and they never pulled the trigger on said trip. Now, ten years later, Andrew Ristow, Charlie Gieseke, and Joe Coleman are taking their weekends to travel around Nebraska to complete their goal of eating pie in every county.

They officially began their travels in February 2018 and have since visited seventeen counties. This past weekend they added to that number by visiting Phelps, Gosper, Frontier, Hayes, and Chase Counties. They arrived at th McKillip Guest House on Saturda afternoon and tried slices of p prepared by Su Cindy Mckillip. to choose betw late Pie and a l **article con**

Ninety-Three Countless Bi
cont..

Before they ate any pie they laid three cards on the table. When asked why they were doing that they explained that it was part of their rules. Anytime there was more than one option of pie they had to draw to see who could pick first. This weekend Joe's card was turned over first! They also explained then that whoever was drawn first had to flip a coin to see who picked next. This time Charlie was second and Andrew third. Joe chose the white chocolate, Charlie also chose the white chocolate, and Andrew was left with the peanut butter pie.

They have even come up with a way to rate the pie they have tasted! Their ranking system is based on a four category 1 to 5 scale. Filling, Crust, Appearance, and Overall taste. They plan to rate every pie they taste throughout their journey and hope to one day document everything. Joe said, "Maybe we will someday turn it into a book."

Goal is to eat pie in every county in Nebr

By Ray Kappel
News Editor

Mmmm...who doesn't like good pie?

How about eating five a day on a road trip? That's what three friends from Lincoln are doing. They aim to eat a pie in every county in Nebraska. That's 93 pies.

Why are they doing? Outside of something fun to do, they don't really know. They got the idea about 10 years ago when they dined at an out of the way café in Lincoln. The pie was delicious and they started thinking. How cool would it be to go on a road trip to eat pies?

The three friends are Joe Coleman, A.J. Ristow, and Charlie Gieseke.

They have already made their Pawnee County stop, Jeannie's in Lewiston. They found the place by googling it on the internet. They use that method or call county clerks and ask for recommendations.

They were glad to find Jeannie's, Joe said.

"That was the best of the day," he said. "I doubt if we find a place better than Jeannie's."

At Jeannie's they had pecan and strawberry rhubarb. They sampled both, Joe said.

They stopped at the Six-Mile Café

The pie eaters are, from left, Joe Coleman, Charlie C AJ Ristow

in Richardson County where Joe got his first taste of sour cream raisin pie. Jeannie Tegtmeier told him later that she makes that pie, too.

"I guess it is not uncommon, but that was the first time I had it," Joe said.

So what about you guys' waistlines, Joe was asked. Well, that could be a problem. When they were out last it was too cold to exercise. At least that's what they say.

Joe wondered if they shoul to each county as a way of off calories. Nah, we'll driv will keep exercise in mind

The five counties they d area were the first of their They have 88 to go and fig out about once a month.

"We should be done in a half," Joe said.

From the Fro
by Bob Bea

Our Webster County S
Clerk, Liz Petsch, called 2
me the other day. Seems O
as though a fellow called r
her and inquired as to who A
in Red Cloud could line m
up a visit from him and a a
traveling companion.
Their goal is to eat a piece w
of pie in every county in o
Nebraska. b

I don't know if this f
will go down in the sl
Guinness Book of World w
Records but it deserves fr
some attention and looking into. c
The Moonstone v
Bookstore is going to
sponsor this event a

not on
ie they
, as the
in Lin-
vorks for
lispatch
ght shop
: school
s before
for him
ctrician
es to be
ext four
for Mo-
anages
tores in
store is
viduals
abilities
e and a

McKil-
ey still
o Chase
nd then
call it
d head

— Across Nebras

Bob
ived an
it from
Webster
A person
nch was
ould put
th some-
r County
a pic for
eems like
quest.
the rest of
were in a
a piece of
Nebraska's
document
of location
occur, and
ed.
Beardslee
called it he
ed if he
I someone
d like it
fun event,
s said soft-

THE PIE . . . ALA MODE — left to right, Bob Beardslee,
Ristow, Charlie Gieseke, and Moonstone Bookstore and
Pottie Osborne. Photos—Ron Bartels

we knew the pie
was probably on.
e all a little pre-
when there young
ered the Bookstore,
a pie hungry look
faces?
introductions all
d around and as
n sat down to a
the tables for a
g THAT PIE, all
sing men needed in
nt as one of them
g. "This in the
reception we have
eived and by far
presentation of the
f pie."
three very cordial
en soon explained
a pie thing was
a co-operative
I three were native
is, but as college
es they were
kicking around
something to do
Collectively they
s to all 48 states.
not something in
d? A reason to see
in all of the
of Nebraska?
s mentioned that
sked pie, and the
bom.
er, college grad-
ate and went and
rtie Gieske is a
arrived at the agreed upon

Please see LANGE-KUBICK, Page A5

NICOLE NERI, JOURNAL STAR

Andrew Ristow (from left), Joe Coleman and Charlie Gieseke pose Sunday with the Trapper Keeper, the official record book of their pie-judging
journey through every county in Nebraska.

In search of a perfect slice

The Pie Guys were college roommates who started talking loose and fast about eating pie a dozen years ago.

A lot of pie.

More pie than Village Inn keeps in that cooler by the cash register. More pie than your grandma and all your aunts make for the annual church bake sale.

**CINDY
LANGE-KUBICK**

More pies than a Hooker County cow pasture.

The Pie Guys are in their 30s now. Charlie Gieseke and Andrew Ristow met back in elementary school, and Ristow and Joe Coleman worked together at Super Saver in high school.

They were all live music lovers who took road trips to listen to their favorite bands.

They (apparently) also liked pie.

So they dreamed up a road trip to all 93 counties — one massive piefest — forking up

flaky crust and fruit filling in every corner of Nebraska.

It didn't happen before their lease expired and they tossed their tassels, but every once in a while, they'd resurrect the grand plan.

And then let it drop.

But last Thanksgiving — the de facto national day of pie — they decided to just do it.

"There's really not a good story behind it," Gieseke says. "We just wanted to have fun with friends and eat pie."

And on an icy Saturday in late February, they set out in Coleman's 1998 Corolla with the goal of hitting a half-dozen Southeast Nebraska counties.

They slipped and slid their way out of Lincoln and headed

to Stop 1, Mary's Cafe in Nebraska City.

They scooted over to Auburn next, then Dawson, then Tecumseh and, finally, to Jeannie's Place in Lewiston, a tiny village of 60 in Pawnee County, before calling it a day.

In the months since, the Pie Guys have eaten heavenly pies and freezer-burned pies; cream pies

and fruit pies and nut pies, pies that could not be redeemed with ice cream and pies they'll never forget.

Like the pies at Jeannie's Place, where Coleman and Ristow sampled pecan pie a la mode and Gieseke sat down to a piece of strawberry rhubarb.

"Vicious rhubarb," he said.

Jeannie Tegtmeier remembers her out-of-town visitors that icy Saturday, too.

"I have a little cafe in my home," the retired teacher said. "I was surprised they came because the weather wasn't very good."

Pleasant young men, she called the Pie Guys. "I imagine they're still at it."

Indeed, they are.

lown of what
are doing!'"
l news is,
ks are helpful
hey don't want
ounty that lets

00 miles to the
s County Clerk
rsmith replied to
email and wel-
trio to town in

the town's only
be closed that
'he'd baked a
ter pie. Cindy

ersmith said Monday.
"Their story was fun."

So fun that that story ended up in the local paper and now the Pie Guys are headed back west for the county fair with their old-school Trapper Keeper and their pie-scoring sheets.

(Pies are rated on a scale of 1-5 for taste, filling, crust and visual appeal. No pie has yet earned a perfect 20, but Jeannie's came close.)

Hayes County may very well have its own rating system, but either way, the

be 40 or 50 pies," Messersmith said. "They (the Pie Guys) will be full."

Full and happy.

"This is more than I ever wanted," Gieseke said. "This is great."

And the Pie Guys want you to know they didn't sit down with a reporter just to get their picture in the paper.

Been there, done that.

But they do need one thing, Coleman said.

"Recommendations for pie."

LEG #9

A NEW CONTENDER

4/13/19 —————————— **407 Miles**

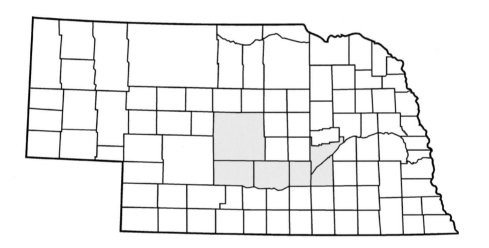

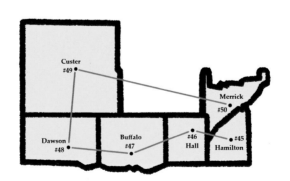

A beautiful day from start to finish? Could this really be Pie-braska? Exactly one year after the chaos that was Superstorm Xanto, we made our earliest start yet for another six stop run. The day would give us two historic Pies... for very different reasons. AJ began yet again with a full breakfast, something he would soon be regretting after four consecutive Cream Pies.

Rath's Cafe in Aurora was our first, thanks to Jessica's recommendation for Hamilton County during Leg #7. With it came our first Lemon Cream (the welcome difference being a topping of homemade whipped cream instead of the usual meringue), which catapulted into the upper echelon of Charlie's ranks. This helped us realize that until Rath's, nearly all of Charlie's favorite Pies had been Rhubarb of one sort or another, which naturally caused him to refer to himself as "Rhubarb the red-nosed Piedeer." The response that followed in the back seat came from a hazy-eyed and recently sleeping AJ. "Piedeer? Is that the name of the ethanol plant?" I can't explain why any of this happened, but will file it under "More great work from the Pie Guys."

Grand Island's Farmer's Daughter Cafe in Hall County brought some varied ratings across the board, but was unanimously chosen as our favorite stop of the day. We met Deb, who runs the place. Deb has a daughter and a horse. I know this because she mistook AJ for her daughter, and said Charlie reminded her of her horse (who shares his name). The place was packed, everyone was personable and we had a nice chat with the table next to us about Pie-braska. After Charlie posed as a butterfly (true story) we were off. Things were going without a hitch... until we passed through the town of Shelton. As it turns out, going faster than the posted speed limit is against the law (who knew?!). Officer Clark of the Shelton Police Dept was also made aware of this at some point in his training, and subsequently pulled us over for said offense. When asked where we were heading and for what, our reply caused an unexpected chuckle for Clark (as it often does), who confessed he hadn't heard that one before. He expressed his desire for a piece of Pie in exchange for the warning he eventually handed me, but unfortunately we were only traveling toward some, not with any. We invited him to follow us the

The warning

63

remaining 20 miles to Buffalo County and our next slice, but he apparently had more pressing matters at hand.

The Lodge in Kearney brought a nice round of Pies (the scores don't reflect how interesting they were) baked by Sabrina, our waitress. We asked her three or four times to tell us the name of Charlie's Milk Chocolate Sweetened Condensed Pie so we'd notate it correctly, which was another first for Pie-braska. Leaving The Lodge however, our main talking point was the inevitable overflow of the toilet in their men's room... yeesh. On our way to Lexington, and during AJ's 12th nap of the morning, Charlie and I counted the usual "friendly" highway cars who gave an acknowledging wave as we passed each other. This was prompted by my being too late to reciprocate a wave, which I overcompensated for by giving them to every vehicle that followed. 33 waves later I finally got one back. You've got some serious self-reflection to do Buffalo and Dawson Counties.

Enter the 48th Pie. It was a sight to behold, earning a perfect visual rating from all. Beyond that, it was a kind of Coconut Pie we hadn't encountered before (Toasted). It was a monster. It's the kind of Pie you write home to your wife about in wartime. No, this did not get a perfect 20 from anybody, and yes, other Pies have earned that distinction without this kind of preamble. But there was just something about this beast of a Pie that seemed special and otherworldly to me. The fact that it nearly killed AJ due to his cream intake up to that point made it even better. Mataya, the proud maker and owner of Madeline's Cafe & Bakery in Lexington, said she usually satisfies an entire women's group with one piece! Evidently, our grading has gotten stricter as we're now past the halfway point, and were it not for a slight crust discrepancy this may have landed atop the pile.

The rest of the day included me asking the guys and our waitress what a patty melt was and not getting an answer from either, some average Pie and some not exactly average Pie. At our momentous 50th stop in Merrick County, Barb Paup of Central City was extremely generous to meet us at her already closed diner to complete our trip after business hours. We rushed in and out so she could still make her granddaughter's recital, powering through our last piece. Today hurt more than usual, but we loved every minute of it.

QUOTES OUT OF CONTEXT

"What was that?!" - Joe;
"What?" - Charlie;
"I was talking to my mouth." - Joe

"Bring me a glass of clotted beer milk." - Charlie

THINGS WE LEARNED

If you turn left you're going west, no matter what.

Too much sugar hurts sometimes.

SPOTLIGHT:
Madeline's Café & Bakery
Lexington, Dawson County

Feminine energy. This is how Mataya Schwarz, the owner, describes the vibe at Madeline's. It is not a place you go to catch the big game on a flat screen. It is where you go to enjoy something truly unique, whether sampling the treats or an expertly curated lunch special. Mataya sees herself and the baristas at Madeline's as modern day hairdressers. Every day they hear about customers' wins, losses and life stories, turning them into makeshift counselors and therapists... all during the time it takes to make a cup of coffee. At times, this can include just Mataya and her mom, affectionately known to locals as "the girls."

Madeline's history may not be a long one, but time is all this newest incarnation lacks (the building itself is the second oldest in town, and one of only three left standing after the Lexington fire of 1890). Since opening in 2008, it has had 4 different owners (all of them women), Mataya being the most recent, acquiring the building in 2018. The name was a tribute to the first owner's grandmother, who ran a restaurant called the Red Rooster Cafe in a nearby town many years ago, and Mataya felt that connection needed to remain a part of the Cafe's future. Her version of Madeline's contains recipes that have been handed down through each transition, but she has also added her own flavors and ideas into the mix, including gluten-free options for nearly all offerings. Mataya comes from a family that has always bonded over food, something she has infused into the Cafe.

Born and raised in Lexington, Mataya doesn't describe it as a "touristy town," but she thinks there's something for everyone to enjoy. The Dawson County History Museum is a great starting point, where you can get a real flavor of the region from folks most passionate about the subject. On the outskirts you'll find Mac's Creek Winery & Brewery, where you can tour the vineyard for tastings and maybe catch some live music. There are multiple parks in Lexington, as well as a one-screen movie theater run by volunteers (mostly local students, who have also taken on the decade-long task of renovating it so they can continue showing first run features for years to come). Lexington is a wonderful community that Mataya has seen change for the better in her time living there, with expanding diversity and an ability to incorporate many different cultures into a small space.

Mataya's favorite part of running the Cafe is when she gets to place whatever is freshly baked into the display case, causing audible whispers of excitement all around. Surely no item elicits more goosebumps upon arrival than Madeline's previously mentioned go to specialty, the Toasted Coconut Pie. A perennial favorite, this Pie always tops the list of pre-order requests for family Thanksgivings in Dawson County and beyond. In spite of this masterpiece, Mataya held firm to her personal feelings that nothing beats an Apple Pie. Fully willing to divulge her own preference, Mataya was also kind enough to share the recipe for my favorite, the famed Toasted Coconut. Some secrets are too good to be kept.

THE REGULAR:
Linda Moore

Linda's history with Madeline's goes back to well before it was around, when she used to frequent the Red Rooster just outside of town, run by Madeline herself. She appreciates that original recipes have been handed down and are still used, even if tweaked, at Madeline's in the present day (although she doesn't lament the exclusion of the original famous calf fries at the Rooster). Linda comes for the atmosphere, and loves supporting a local business. Whether it's for a meeting, a church function, or simply to sit with friends, Linda appreciates Mataya's ability to provide a space for anything and everything. When I asked her what are some of her favorite items at Madeline's, she applauded the soup, sandwiches and wraps, but not before her response of "Are you kidding me? I come for the sweets!" High honors of course went to the Pie, as well as their lavender cupcakes (an item she hasn't had elsewhere). But the top prize for Linda has to go to Madeline's Cookie Cups, a chocolate chip cookie baked in a muffin tin and stuffed with chocolate ganache. Her sales pitch was that while her son was training for an overseas military deployment, his entire unit made a trip to Lexington in a Chinook helicopter, exclusively to pick up a batch of Cookie Cups. Sold.

#45 Hamilton County - Rath's Cafe (Aurora) @ 7:30 AM - $3.00

	Filling	Crust	Visual	Taste	Total	Type
AJ	5	3	5	4	17	Peanut Butter
Charlie	5	3	5	5	18	Lemon Cream
Joe	5	3	4	5	17	Cherry
					17.33	

#46 Hall County - Farmer's Daughter Cafe (Grand Island) @ 8:20 AM - $2.79   BEST

	Filling	Crust	Visual	Taste	Total	Type
AJ	2	1	1	3	7	Chocolate Meringue
Charlie	3	3	1	5	12	Strawberry Rhubarb
Joe	4	3	5	5	17	Peanut Butter (w/ whipped cream)
					12	

#47 Buffalo County - The Lodge Restaurant (Kearney) @ 10:02 AM - $4.00

	Filling	Crust	Visual	Taste	Total	Type
AJ	4	1	1	4	10	Coconut Cream
Charlie	4	4	5	4	17	Milk Chocolate Sweetened Condensed
Joe	4	4	3	4	15	Apple
					14	

#48 Dawson County - Madeline's Cafe & Bakery (Lexington) @ 11:12 AM - $3.69

	Filling	Crust	Visual	Taste	Total	Type
AJ	5	4	5	4	18	Toasted Coconut
Charlie	5	4	5	5	19	Toasted Coconut
Joe	5	3	5	5	18	Toasted Coconut
					18.33	

#49 Custer County - Tumbleweed Cafe (Broken Bow) @ 12:58 PM - $2.95

	Filling	Crust	Visual	Taste	Total	Type
AJ	3	2	3	3	11	Cherry
Charlie	2	3	4	3	12	Blueberry
Joe	4	3	4	4	15	Sour Cream & Raisin
					12.67	

#50 Merrick County - Mom & Paup Family Restaurant (Central City) @ 3:25 PM - $3.00

	Filling	Crust	Visual	Taste	Total	Type
AJ	2	1	4	1	8	Apple
Charlie	2	1	3	1	7	Apple
Joe	2	1	3	1	7	Apple
					7.33	

Hamilton County

Busted

Joe & Deb at Farmer's Daughter

Rath's Café

It had to be done

Peanut Butter at Farmer's Daughter

Eating Pie after hours

Toasted Coconut at Madeline's

I PLEDGE ALLEGIANCE TO THE PUDDING

5/11/19 ——————————— **189 Miles**

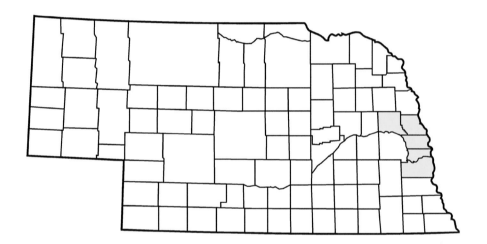

Scores were low. Miles were low. Tension was high. I was thrilled to start my day with a Banana Cream (historically my favorite) which has proven itself a rarity throughout Pie-braska, but on this day was anything but. This was our "big city" run for all intents and purposes, as we meandered through Omaha and surrounding areas, which definitely had a different vibe in comparison with earlier outings. On the whole, not much of the day would be embedded in my long term memory. One exception would be the dispute in Sarpy County...

Our biggest divide yet came at the hands of the Downtown Coffee Shop's Banana Cream Pie in Bellevue. With our unspoken rule to not discuss our thoughts until leaving, we were all under the assumption that each of our respective reactions would be met with the same happy fervor or disillusionment from the others. Since I'm the one fortunate enough to be writing this, I will selfishly relay my thoughts only. The look wasn't perfect, yet at the same time strangely appealing as it was clearly not store-bought or molded on an assembly line. It was so unlike the previous Banana Cream I had only an hour earlier, as well as all others. To me, the consistency was perfect, and I'm sure my eyes lit up after my first bite. Trying to keep my excitement under wraps, I eagerly awaited the jaunt to our third stop, where we could collectively revel in its greatness. Much to my surprise and chagrin, when I began by awarding the filling a 5, both AJ and Charlie erupted in shock. There's not a lot else to go into here and I won't claim this Pie was without flaw (as you can see should you care to pore through the ratings chart), but on a short run this divergence of thought ruled the remainder of the day. The following week I gave my best investigative effort to dispel the rumor that it was simply pudding on a crust, suggested (loudly and often) by AJ. I spoke with Cindy at the Downtown who said the Pies are homemade by the owner, Chris. She expanded, saying the crusts are made with lard, and the mix used is from their supplier (which she said is similar to a pudding mix but is not) before fresh bananas are added (which I will admit could have been more plentiful).

I will grant that taking this step was highly unusual since we never claim to be experts, nor do we require knowing the nuts and bolts of any given Pie. And while we surely have disagreements, this big of an imbalance hasn't been seen since the great Hayes County Fair Pecan debacle, so it most definitely warranted further exploration. I realize there's nothing I could have discovered that would change the opinions and tastes of the others because, if the Pie don't fit... But I do take solace in the fact that these were mixed and baked in house, which gives them more legitimacy than many, regardless of personal preference. I mean, aren't all Cream Pies basically a pudding mix? It was delicious.

...oh yeah, there were hundreds of Corvettes at The Rustic in Fort Calhoun, AJ had a Pie crust not dissimilar to sand, and Joe's Cafe served their Pie with a spoon on a plate (an Omaha thing?). All firsts.

QUOTES OUT OF CONTEXT

"Let it rain on him, eat it up with a spoon." - Charlie (singing)

THINGS WE LEARNED

AJ doesn't like pudding.

AJ doesn't like sand.

LEG #10 (5/11/19)

#51 Cass County - Mom's Cafe & Catering (Plattsmouth) @ 7:50 AM - $4.25

	Filling	Crust	Visual	Taste	Total	Type
AJ	3	3	4	3	13	Raisin Cream
Charlie	4	3	2	4	13	Lemon
Joe	3	4	4	3	14	Banana Cream
					13.33	

#52 Sarpy County - Downtown Coffee Shop (Bellevue) @ 8:35 AM - $3.10

	Filling	Crust	Visual	Taste	Total	Type
AJ	3	3	2	2	10	Banana Cream
Charlie	3	2	3	2	10	Banana Cream
Joe	5	3	3	5	16	Banana Cream
					12	

#53 Douglas County - Joe's Cafe (Omaha) @ 9:28 AM - $2.75

	Filling	Crust	Visual	Taste	Total	Type
AJ	4	3	4	4	15	Key Lime
Charlie	4	3	2	2	11	Peanut Butter
Joe	3	2	3	3	11	Banana Cream
					12.33	

#54 Washington County - The Rustic (Fort Calhoun) @ 10:14 AM - $3.69 `BEST`

	Filling	Crust	Visual	Taste	Total	Type
AJ	3	1	3	2	9	Coconut Cream
Charlie	4	2	2	3	11	Apple
Joe	4	3	4	4	15	French Silk
					11.67	

#55 Dodge County - Mac's Cafe (Fremont) @ 11:54 AM - $1.89

	Filling	Crust	Visual	Taste	Total	Type
AJ	2	3	3	3	11	Chocolate Vanilla Cream
Charlie	2	3	4	2	11	Chocolate Nestle Crunch
Joe	3	5	4	3	15	Root Beer Float
					12.33	

Cass County

Downtown Coffee Shop

Pies displayed at Mac's

Joe's Café

Doing what he does

Banana Cream at Downtown Coffee Shop

Pure muscle

Still angry about the Banana Cream

LEG #11

PIEHENGE

7/26/19 - 7/28/19 ——————————— **1,115 Miles**

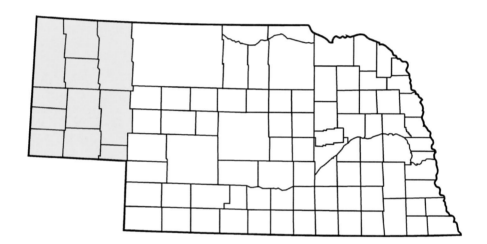

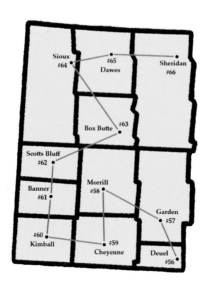

This was the big one. The run we'd been anticipating from the beginning, poised to stamp our biggest checkmark yet on the mammoth Panhandle of Nebraska. Nearly doubling in distance our longest leg to date and taking up the entire weekend to do so, we were sure to encounter some all-time slices. We were right... just not as often as we'd like to have been.

It was well spread out, with one slice on Friday night, five on Saturday, and five more on Sunday. There were only one or two hiccups, both easily handled to make it a full and fairly smooth weekend. In Garden County's Oshkosh, Ryan Martinez at the Patriot Grill brought us one of those magical slices that do not come along often, showing us what Strawberry Rhubarb can be. You know how the name of a Pie tends to give the eater an idea of the ingredients contained therein? Well, this was the first Strawberry Rhubarb I'd ever had that held spectacularly true to its title. Both were so well represented and so perfectly done, it was a revelation. This wasn't our first incredible Pie coming from someone who doesn't bake them on the regular, which begs the question... why? Talking with Ryan was great, who genuinely tried to stop AJ from ordering the breakfast burrito, knowing we had four more pieces of Pie ahead of us on the day. AJ didn't heed the warning, and a burrito roughly the size of a barge arrived some minutes later. Naturally he cleaned his plate, holding steadfast to his creed of never going without a breakfast, Pie run be damned. Even still, Ryan informed us our money was no good there, expressing his happiness in seeing others follow a passion and doing what they loved. Next up was another homemade Strawberry Rhubarb not typically on the menu, and another owner (of Bridgeport's Call Me Cupcake in Morrill County) refusing to accept payment for such wonders. Grandma Jo's in Cheyenne County's Sidney was not in the same charitable mood as they knocked us back into reality... without a smile... we'll be fine.

The remainder of Saturday gave us more nice stops, a beautiful drive, and we were able to take in the Scotts Bluff National Monument to walk off some of our recently acquired heft. We had a warm welcome from family in Gering to recharge for the long push home the following morning. Before we were able to take in our Sunday morning Pie with the fam, disappointment was sprung on us at our planned destination. "I was told the Pie was for July 28th," remarked the shop's owner... before realizing it was that very day. Whoops. Thankfully we were with locals, and were quickly ushered to Shari's across the bridge in Scottsbluff, where multiple varieties of Pie are always on hand (including a

Marionberry, another new one for us not often found in the Midwest). While at Shari's, our travels were discussed at length, a topic not easily avoided the further we went. As we recited lore from various Pie excursions pre-dating the current, it included bakers refusing to divulge coveted recipes that created some of the best tastes we'd found. We were told of similar legends in the neighboring town of Gering, like the woman who took her recipe to the grave (literally) and had it etched on the back of her tombstone, and of certain cakes so renowned and sought after that when it was heard they would be appearing at gatherings, attendance would quickly double or triple.

Finding Pie in the northwest corner of Nebraska on a Sunday wasn't the easiest task, exhibit A being our Box Butte stop at the Alliance Grocery Kart. This was our best option after weeks of planning and trying to nail something down other than a grocery store, but here we were again. The pre-packaged Pies were about as expected, but there were multiple options so it was agreed we would all buy our own full Pie to take to Carhenge (which is still in the county... there are rules after all). If you ever make it down that way, look for our signature on the car (you'll know which one). To close it out we had two more firsts for Pie-braska, Pistachio and Fruit of the Forest, but aside from that nothing otherworldly to report from either offering. Dawes County is who wowed us on our way back home...

It's getting harder and harder to really impress us with one of the single fruit standards (Apple, Cherry or Peach), but the Bean Broker in Chadron did it. Their Peach was a sight to behold and a wonder to taste. We had the luxury of seeing the full Pie before it was served, lattice top and all. Of course we still rated the visual on the slice as presented, but this was a nice primer. Yes it scored well, but somehow didn't land high enough to clearly show the tier it was to be placed in (the top one). The peaches were unlike any others I'd had in a Pie (or outside of one frankly), retaining the juicy crisp and rough edge even after the bake, and the homemade whipped cream added another dimension. Phenomenal. It was my first visit to Chadron, and provided a great reason to not be my last. Afterward, Charlie did his best Elton John impression just two blocks away... look for it on the cover of his debut album, Empty Pie.

QUOTES OUT OF CONTEXT

"It's called a cherry burn." - AJ

"I ate what I thought I ate!" - Joe

THINGS WE LEARNED

Taste is always a five.

Strawberry Rhubarb Pie can have real strawberries
and real rhubarb in it.

AJ is no fan of a Pinterest interior.

SPOTLIGHT:
The Patriot Grill
Oshkosh, Garden County

On July 18th, 2018, Ryan and Dana Martinez officially opened the doors of
The Patriot Grill. This was the latest of many leaps of faith taken by Ryan on
his way to this moment. Originally from Miami, Florida, where he raised three
kids, Ryan came to Oshkosh years ago to visit his brother. After leaving for
home, a deal was made with his brother that he would move to Oshkosh if a
house could be found for $20,000. He wound up returning shortly thereafter
when his brother did exactly that. There was no safety net to catch Ryan as
he moved his family 2,000 miles from home, not knowing exactly how they
would land. Securing a job at Cabela's where he met Dana, his future wife, they
spent the next 14 years putting down roots. Fast forward to 2015, and Ryan's
previous restaurant experience from his years in Colorado became known to
Oshkosh's owner of Panhandler's Pizza and Subs, who reached out and asked
if he'd be willing to help out when he could. Ryan jumped in feet first, eventually
leading to the opportunity to lease the building and run Panhandler's for its
final year in 2017. Not long after, he bought it outright and changed the name,
menu and atmosphere to turn it into The Patriot Grill of today.

Ryan talks of immediately being taken by how nice the people of Oshkosh and Nebraska at large had been upon moving in, making him feel as if he were born and raised there. He happily recalls all of the friendly "one-finger waves" he was so struck by on the roads of Oshkosh, in stark contrast to a very different kind of "one-finger wave" he had gotten used to in Miami. The only hurdle that took some time to clear was becoming a Husker fan (something not so easily done for a guy born and raised in Brighton, Colorado, where Buffalo fans reign), but after some steady prodding from an Oshkosh local, he mustered the will to make the conversion.

You can't talk to Ryan very long without being made aware of his immense pride in what he does at The Patriot Grill. He will tell you how his locally famous prime rib night is frequented weekly by people from all around Nebraska and even Colorado, and that the origin of its well regarded status was handed down to him by an old mentor in the food business. He is equally proud of his peppercorn brandy over beef medallions, which he found success with early on as it aided him on the dating scene as a young man. Another feather in his cap is how he keeps egg rolls on hand for one customer who eats them exclusively, but comes in weekly with her husband who eats everything else. There are more stories than will fit in this modest showcase for Ryan and The Patriot Grill, but he would be glad to tell you any of them if you're able to make the trip his way.

Pie is not always featured on the menu, but if you're lucky enough to get the chance, don't pass it up. We had his personal favorite, Strawberry Rhubarb, and I will take this opportunity to recommend it again. The personal connection for Ryan and this Pie goes back to his grandma making it when he was younger, and having a rhubarb plant in his own backyard that he would take stalks from to dip in the sugar bowl. Another nod to Ryan's roots that is immediately evident when sitting in The Patriot Grill is his respect for the military. Ryan is an Army Veteran himself, offering discounts to those actively serving in any branch, as well as the men and women who have done so previously.

THE REGULAR:
Dwain Sutton

Ryan describes Dwain as an original cowboy, saying he's been coming into Oshkosh for 55 years, and he used to do it with two guns on his hips. In talking with Dwain about what makes The Patriot Grill special to him, he kept it very simple. "It's a nice place and I like Ryan." I know the first part to be true, and the second is easy to believe. Dwain drops in two or three times each week, and has lived in Oshkosh and the surrounding area his whole life. Part of his felt connection to the place may date back to being a "submarine guy" in the Navy, and Ryan has made those who've served feel a natural part of things when they walk in his front door. "It was a welcome change," Dwain commented when asked about The Patriot Grill in comparison to what stood there previously. He saw a whole new attitude shift when Ryan took over and transformed it into what it is today, and Dwain will keep coming back.

LEG #11 (7/26/19 - 1/28/19)

7/26/19 (1 stop)

#56 Deuel County - Max's Highway Diner (Big Springs) @ 8:50 PM - $3.25

	Filling	Crust	Visual	Taste	Total	Type
AJ	2	3	2	3	10	Cherry
Charlie	3	2	3	3	11	Blueberry
Joe	3	3	3	2	11	Peach
					10.67	

7/27/19 (5 stops)

#57 Garden County - The Patriot Grill (Oshkosh) @ 9:00 AM - $0.00   **BEST**

	Filling	Crust	Visual	Taste	Total	Type
AJ	5	5	3	5	18	Strawberry Rhubarb
Charlie	5	4	2	5	16	Strawberry Rhubarb
Joe	5	5	3	5	18	Strawberry Rhubarb
					17.33	

#58 Morrill County - Call Me Cupcake (Bridgeport) @ 10:44 AM - $0.00

	Filling	Crust	Visual	Taste	Total	Type
AJ	3	4	4	4	15	Strawberry Rhubarb
Charlie	3	3	4	3	13	Strawberry Rhubarb
Joe	4	3	4	3	14	Strawberry Rhubarb
					14	

#59 Cheyenne County - Grandma Jo's (Sidney) @ 11:59 AM - $3.25

	Filling	Crust	Visual	Taste	Total	Type
AJ	3	3	3	2	11	Peach
Charlie	2	3	3	2	10	Strawberry Rhubarb
Joe	3	3	4	2	12	Chocolate Meringue
					11	

#60 Kimball County - The Diner (Kimball) @ 1:15 PM - $3.95

	Filling	Crust	Visual	Taste	Total	Type
AJ	3	4	2	3	12	Apple (w/ whipped cream)
Charlie	2	4	3	4	13	Peach (w/ whipped cream)
Joe	2	3	5	2	12	Pumpkin (w/ whipped cream)
					12.33	

#61 Banner County - Laura Lee's Double L Cafe (Harrisburg) @ 2:15 PM - $3.50

	Filling	Crust	Visual	Taste	Total	Type
AJ	4	4	4	4	16	French Coconut
Charlie	1	2	2	2	7	Peaches And Cream
Joe	4	3	2	3	12	Blueberry
					11.67	

7/28/19 (5 stops)

#62 Scotts Bluff County - Shari's Cafe And Pies (Scottsbluff) @ 9:40 AM - $3.99 ***WC***

	Filling	Crust	Visual	Taste	Total	Type
AJ	3	3	3	3	12	Sour Cream Lemon
Charlie	2	1	3	3	9	Butterscotch
Joe	4	2	3	5	14	Marionberry
					11.67	

#63 Box Butte County - Alliance Grocery Kart (Alliance) @ 12:00 PM - $4.99

	Filling	Crust	Visual	Taste	Total	Type
AJ	3	3	4	1	11	Pumpkin
Charlie	2	2	3	3	10	Strawberry Rhubarb
Joe	4	3	3	3	13	Cherry
					11.33	

#64 Sioux County - Sandcreek Cookhouse (Crawford) @ 2:15 PM - $4.00

	Filling	Crust	Visual	Taste	Total	Type
AJ	4	3	3	5	15	Pecan
Charlie	2	1	3	2	8	Pumpkin
Joe	4	3	4	4	15	Pistachio
					12.67	

#65 Dawes County - Bean Broker Coffee House And Pub (Chadron) @ 3:35 PM - $4.00

	Filling	Crust	Visual	Taste	Total	Type
AJ	5	3	3	5	16	Peach (w/ whipped cream)
Charlie	5	3	3	5	16	Peach (w/ whipped cream)
Joe	5	4	3	5	17	Peach (w/ whipped cream)
					16.33	

#66 Sheridan County - Antelope Creek Cafe (Gordon) @ 4:55 PM - $2.95

	Filling	Crust	Visual	Taste	Total	Type
AJ	5	3	4	4	16	Blueberry
Charlie	3	2	3	2	10	Fruit Of The Forest
Joe	4	5	3	4	16	Apple
					14	

Garden County

Sandcreek Cookhouse

What else did you expect?

Carhenge

Leaving our mark

Strawberry Rhubarb at The Patriot

Blazing the trail

Empty Pie

LEG #12
MOON PIES

10/12/19 ———————————— **443 Miles**

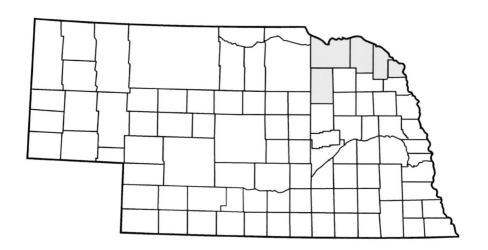

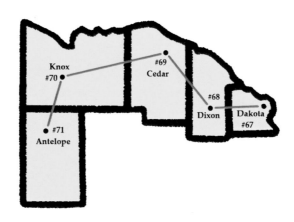

When my windshield calls for the first frost scraping of the season... I know it's time for a Pie run. We started this one early to make it to the northeast corner of the state for another scamper along the border, beginning in Dakota County. When we landed in South Sioux City, we found out Brian from the Crystal Cafe had started even earlier. In talking with our waitress after enjoying a delicious opening to our trip, we found that he bakes a fresh variety of Pies for the Cafe at 3:00 AM every single day. Thank you Brian, I hope we can shake your hand some day. Before even ordering we sat in the booth nearest the Pie cooler (as you do) and were awestruck at the Sour Cream Raisin that demanded our full attention. The meringue was domed, reaching heights of roughly 6 feet (I'm not good at estimates). I was lucky enough to win the first draw of the day, quickly making that my choice. Removing one slice from the dome seemed a precarious endeavor, and as the plate was set on our table, my Pie resembled the roof of the Sydney Opera House. The others looked great too, all scoring well in one area or many.

All online info for Henry's in Allen is followed by parentheses containing "formerly the Village Inn." So when we drove up expecting the standard orange/brown/yellow shell of a building we've seen countless times, you can imagine our surprise and delight to come across Henry's as it is. It must have been a very different Village Inn, because we walked into a rather large warehouse or barn type of structure with 25 foot ceilings. Containing multiple rusted out cars from decades ago and life-size recreations of the Blues Brothers far above our heads, it was definitely a new look alongside our morning Pie. This wasn't our last ambitious building conversion to be seen, which came in the form of Verdigre's Cozy Corner Cafe in Knox County. Their utilitarian half dome turned restaurant created a very simple, straightforward and nice space. The entire staff on-hand was extremely kind and helpful, having baked two Pies for us, and sending us off with the leftovers free of charge (I jumped past Donna's Diner in Cedar County in my excitement to talk about another unorthodox building, so if you'd like a full review of our Pie experience there, please see our first quote from this trip to gain some insight into Charlie's expert analytical approach. What more could you need?).

A rare stop un-related to Pie was made before we hit Green Gables of Pleasant Valley. Could this be?! Had the Pie Guys lost their way? We were now in AJ country, where he spent time as a child at the family farm near Plainview. Fond memories of the sabretooth deer and other fabled creatures such as the giant bone-crushing dog (real thing) were revisited at Ashfall Fossil Beds, just outside of Royal. Turns out fossils don't change much in the span of a couple decades, and we found things just as AJ had left them. And so we landed at stop #71 of Pie-braska in Antelope County. This was one of the truly rare "roadside stops." Technically part of Royal, Green Gables really occupies its own space without a neighbor to claim for itself (much like Dawson's Six Mile Cafe or Laura Lee's in Harrisburg). It doubled as a diner/country store, selling clothes, furniture and trinkets in addition to a beautifully stacked Pie window. This was a fun one, and comes recommended for sure.

Once again we were left with a multi-hour ride home, and stomachs bordering on sickly (which didn't stop us from getting some Arby's sliders in Norfolk... even when we're full there always creeps in a deep desire for something savory on these Pie-filled Saturdays). As AJ took the helm in a rare driver switch, we all marveled at how awesome the moon looked in the early evening heading east. When I claimed preference over the "Great American Eclipse" of 2017 (I seem to be the only human unmoved by the phenomenon), it conjured up memories of our grand rainbow debate during Leg #4 (I think they're rare, AJ and Charlie think otherwise, yet I've only seen one in the year and a half since that day... which happened to be on our last Pie run in Gering!). I guess we have a thing for Pie and the sky.

QUOTES OUT OF CONTEXT

"This is not a surprise... it's a Pumpkin Pie." - Charlie

"It's a flat pile." - AJ

THINGS WE LEARNED

The Pie Gods have turned on AJ.

LEG #12 (10/12/19)

#67 Dakota County - Crystal Cafe (South Sioux City) @ 10:00 AM - $3.99 — BEST

	Filling	Crust	Visual	Taste	Total	Type
AJ	5	4	4	5	18	Cherry
Charlie	3	2	4	4	13	Coconut Cream
Joe	5	3	4	5	17	Sour Cream Raisin
					16	

#68 Dixon County - Henry's (Allen) @ 11:02 AM - $2.00

	Filling	Crust	Visual	Taste	Total	Type
AJ	4	3	3	3	13	Apple
Charlie	3	3	4	3	13	Pecan
Joe	3	3	4	3	13	Pecan
					13	

#69 Cedar County - Donna's Diner (Wynot) @ 12:21 PM - $2.25

	Filling	Crust	Visual	Taste	Total	Type
AJ	4	3	4	3	14	Sour Cream Raisin
Charlie	3	3	3	3	12	Pumpkin (w/ whipped cream)
Joe	3	4	3	3	13	Cherry
					13	

#70 Knox County - Cozy Corner Cafe (Verdigre) @ 1:52 PM - $0.00

	Filling	Crust	Visual	Taste	Total	Type
AJ	3	1	2	3	9	Chocolate
Charlie	3	1	2	3	9	Chocolate
Joe	3	2	4	1	10	Apple
					9.33	

#71 Antelope County - Green Gables Of Pleasant Valley (Royal) @ 3:32 PM - $5.00

	Filling	Crust	Visual	Taste	Total	Type
AJ	4	3	4	5	16	Peanut Butter
Charlie	2	3	4	2	11	Caramel Apple Nut
Joe	3	5	4	4	16	French Silk
					14.33	

"I think Pie can, I think Pie can..."

Green Gables

Inside the Cozy Corner

Insert Pie here

Dixon County

French Silk at Green Gables

Gooooood morning!

Pie board at Green Gables

THIS PIE GUY'S GONNA FLY!

11/8/19 - 11/9/19 —————————————— **639 Miles**

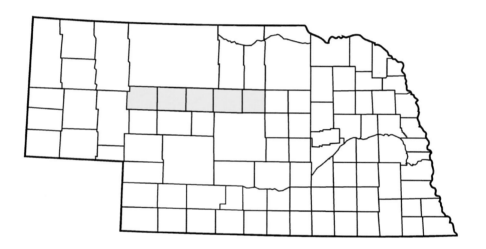

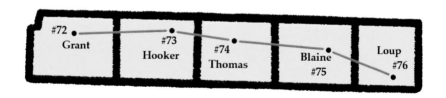

Let's just say some mistakes were made on this trip. The first being to stop for a quick dinner at Applebee's while passing through Grand Island on our way to the Hyannis Hotel. Being perennial suckers for a good deal, we were drawn in by the 25 cent wings (which can only mean quality). Two hours later we left feeling like garbage in human form, passing by countless superior options once north of our questionable choice. This also caused some panic as I phoned the hotel to update them on our timeline, which had me explaining to a third person what we were up to. The clerk simply said "We'll be closed," and was perturbed and confused by our mission (the seriousness of our situation was clearly taken too lightly by the previous two). When I tried explaining further to ensure that Pie from the hotel restaurant would be waiting for us, she replied "You must be bored." In spite of this potential roadblock, it turned out to be no more than a speed bump as we found our room key in the seemingly abandoned hotel, entered our room in Hyannis and found three styrofoam containers on the desk with the necessary contents. Before continuing however, let me first take a step back and tell you about the highlight of Leg #13...

We made just one stop for gas between Grand Island and Hyannis on that Friday night, which was in the previously conquered town of Broken Bow, Custer County. It was at their Casey's convenience store on the town's main drag of Hwy 2 where Charlie and I had a front row seat to one hell of an exhibition. After filling up the tank and putting the Pie mobile in drive to swing around and pick up AJ at the entrance, we saw him exiting the gas station. AJ assumed (understandably) that I was driving away to leave him, and began running in a wide arc to head us off. We stopped the car and enjoyed the show from there. He continued gaining speed coming at us head on, until he was close enough that something altogether new was bound to occur. In a complete show of disrespect for my '98 Corolla, he leaped to plant his left foot on its hood, only to slip on the dust that had accumulated (the shoe print remained for the weekend). Charlie and I watched through the windshield in what seemed like slow motion as his eyes widened, at which point he proceeded to fall to his right and crash into the upper frame of my car before ricocheting off the driver side and slamming into a trash bin. How wonderful it all was. Less wonderful was a Casey's employee shutting me down the following day when I called to try and acquire the security footage, or at least some still images. No pleading was enough to convince her, as she tried to make me aware that security footage is only used for "law enforcement matters." One point retroactively removed from

Custer County.

So we were back on the road to Hyannis and Grant County, narrowly missing a plethora of wildlife in the pitch black, aided only by my underperforming headlights. After a raccoon and skunk barely skirted death, we found ourselves driving parallel with a ghostly looking deer running over a bridge in the lane next to us. It was only noticed through my driver side window once we were next to it, causing me to yell in terror at the shocking image reminiscent of an escaped hospital patient.

After we opened up the futon for Charlie (we drew cards) in Hyannis, creating a definite fire code violation, we ate our Mocha Pie and settled in to rest up for our lowest Pie intake yet (only four slices on a Saturday, what a piece of... Pie). This allowed more leeway as we started our day in Hooker County, so we each got a full breakfast at Red's in Mullen. The precursor to our breakfast was the owner (Red?) telling me in a surly tone "This isn't McDonald's" as I perused the Pie board standing in front of the counter. Not putting in our order within 4 seconds of his arrival at our table also seemed to cause some consternation, so he left after asking what we wanted and before we could answer. Were we really oozing "city folk" that intensely? While their demeanor may not have been, their Pie was above average.

In Thedford's Sandhills Corral of Thomas County, Alicia welcomed us very warmly and prepared what might have been a top tier Pie, but we just didn't catch it on the right day. It tasted delicious and was a new take on Banana Cream (with caramel), but per Alicia's admission, it never really set up properly. She was disappointed and apologized for serving us "pudding," but the effort was appreciated and we enjoyed our stop very much. Next up was an amazing bed and breakfast coming in the form of Uncle Buck's Lodge. Located in Blaine County's town of Brewster, it overlooks the Loup River and endless acres of expanse. We caught Marilyn and the lodge just in time to find their Christmas decorations in full swing. It was something to see, and a place we'd love to revisit. Marilyn sat and talked with us as we ate, regaling us with the history of Uncle Buck's and the tale of the "Sandhills Monkey" (you'll have to ask her yourself).

As we left Loup County and our final stop in Taylor's Lazy D, a woman was walking by outside that we hadn't yet seen, and her first words were "How was the Pie?" We asked her what gave us away, and she told us we just looked like the Pie Guys. When you make it in Taylor, you can make it anywhere.

QUOTES OUT OF CONTEXT

"You can't use the same symbol for crust that you used for consistency!" - AJ

"No one can leave this room... until I decide they can leave this room." - Charlie

THINGS WE LEARNED

Trains are loud.

We found we're even able to argue about calendars.

AJ can wake up at 4:00 am, check the time, tell us the time, and be snoring again all within 10 seconds.

LEG #13 (11/8/19 - 11/9/19)

11/8/19 (1 stop)

#72 Grant County - Hyannis Hotel (Hyannis) @ 11:02 PM (MST) - $3.00

	Filling	Crust	Visual	Taste	Total	Type
AJ	4	1	2	1	8	Mocha
Charlie	3	1	3	2	9	Mocha
Joe	3	2	4	2	11	Mocha
					9.33	

11/9/19 (4 stops)

#73 Hooker County - Red's (Mullen) @ 8:51 AM (MST) - $3.50

	Filling	Crust	Visual	Taste	Total	Type
AJ	4	3	4	5	16	Pecan
Charlie	3	2	3	2	10	Apple
Joe	4	3	4	4	15	Pecan
					13.67	

#74 Thomas County - Sandhills Corral (Thedford) @ 11:22 AM - $1.99

	Filling	Crust	Visual	Taste	Total	Type
AJ	3	3	2	5	13	Caramel Banana Cream
Charlie	3	4	2	5	14	Caramel Banana Cream
Joe	2	3	2	5	12	Caramel Banana Cream
					13	

#75 Blaine County - Uncle Buck's Lodge (Brewster) @ 12:40 PM - $0.00 `BEST`

	Filling	Crust	Visual	Taste	Total	Type
AJ	2	2	2	3	9	Chocolate Cream
Charlie	4	5	4	4	17	Sour Cream Raisin
Joe	4	4	4	4	16	Sour Cream Raisin
					14	

#76 Loup County - Lazy D Restaurant & Lounge (Taylor) @ 1:52 PM - $4.95

	Filling	Crust	Visual	Taste	Total	Type
AJ	3	3	3	3	12	Apple
Charlie	4	3	3	4	14	Apple
Joe	3	3	2	3	11	Apple
					12.33	

Grant County

Red's Café

Making ourselves at home in Uncle Buck's

Hyannis comes through in the clutch

Hyannis Hotel

Close to greatness at Sandhills Corral

Inside Uncle Buck's

Everyone's so nice around here

BROTHER, CAN YOU SPARE A PIE?

2/15/20 ———————————— **295 Miles**

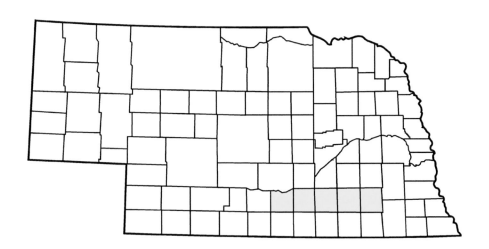

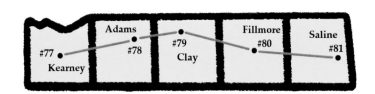

A new decade had begun, yet Pie remained uneaten. As 2020 got underway and we rolled into the homestretch, a sense of completion was in the air as we awoke from our winter Pie-bernation (I'm sorry). Immediately upon walking into Kearney County's South Side Diner of Minden, we were warmly welcomed. Two separate tables engaged us in conversation within seconds, both very inquisitive as to why three strangers were now in their neck of the woods. Our waitress excitedly proclaimed that she had us covered, unveiling multiple Pies behind the counter. We were also lucky enough to arrive around mid-morning as they prepared for their brunch buffet, featuring hot and fresh fried chicken... which we washed down our Pie with. That's when the waitress brought over a basket of candy as a parting gift, as if we hadn't been pampered enough.

A rather exciting moment for me came next, when on our 78th stop I finally got my first Key Lime Pie during this whole thing. It looked great, tasted great, and everything else in the display case at Hastings' Back Alley Bakery of Adams County followed suit. Charlie's Sour Cream Raisin had what he very favorably described as a baklava crust. AJ didn't describe his Coconut at all, outside of it being delicious. Next up was the Legacy Bar & Grill in Harvard, Clay County. We entered with virtually every seating option available, prompting AJ to ask where we wanted to sit. The words of wisdom that followed from Charlie were "Well, we're here for Pie." We sure were. This was a nice stop with a rare mixed berry option, and very friendly owners who were happy we veered off the beaten path to stop in their town. All Pies were courtesy of Cat ("like meow" as she put it), who suggested we make another trip through Nebraska to eat barbecue in each county, promising to provide us with a starting point. That was when the good vibes of the day would take a very serious detour.

The county: Fillmore. The town: Geneva. The establishment: Sister's Cafe. It all began innocently enough as we entered and sat next to an extremely nice local waiting for her carry-out order. To interrupt our brief moment of peace, the waitress approached and asked what we would have. When we told her "Pie," she immediately became incensed and yelled something unintelligible about not being able to do this right now, before storming back to the counter without taking our order. Having no idea what just happened or why, Charlie made a comment to our table mate that we must have come at a bad time. She informed us we had not, and assured us this was standard fare for a trip to Sister's Cafe. As two other locals approached the register so they could be on their way, the cook emerged to yell at them about not eating the Pies she made. None of it was in fun. No jokes were being made. It felt like make believe. As our waitress returned to angrily take our order and give us the Pie options, I ignored Charlie's trembling hands and hesitant disposition, asking that he place the cards on the table for our choices to be determined per the usual routine. Our lovely waitress of course responded with "I ain't touching no cards or doin' NOTHING!" Needless to say this was another first for Pie-braska, so we asked our new friend to help us, who happily obliged. Then we watched the steam come out of our waitress's ears as she waited even longer for us to flip a coin for 2nd choice. When our slices arrived, we did our best to eat them silently and not disturb the fragile ecosphere around us. Amidst all the tension and despair in Fillmore County, after we paid our bills and left I did so without my camera. But lo and behold, who would you guess came out holding it and yelling that I forgot something? Our beloved waitress. We left our 80th stop with the world in balance once again.

The "Czech Capital" of the United States is the town of Wilber, so we decided we should eat Pie there and bowl a few frames to cap our day. The "Detached truck beds for sale sitting in an open field Capital" of the United States appeared to be nearby, also in Saline County. As we passed I told AJ he should shop there (always on the lookout for a welcomed addition to his ailing pickups) and he responded, "Damn dude, I ain't kidding." Right. Judy and Brian of Wil-Bol Lanes invited us inside before opening, where we chatted for some time about their recent acquisition of it and plans for the future. They were kind enough to open a lane for us after we had Judy's homemade Pie, where we decided the loser would foot the bill. I don't want to get into our specific, scores, but let's just say AJ and I didn't have to pay. Wait, maybe that's a little too obvious... Charlie knocked down less pins than we did.

QUOTES OUT OF CONTEXT

"Did you say 'stay home?'" - Charlie;
"He said 'say hough!'" - AJ

"Boy don't want no white on his meringue." - AJ

THINGS WE LEARNED

Some people are angry people.

LEG #14 (2/15/20)

#77 Kearney County - South Side Diner (Minden) @ 9:05 AM - $2.00

	Filling	Crust	Visual	Taste	Total	Type
AJ	2	3	2	3	10	Strawberry Rhubarb
Charlie	3	4	4	3	14	Apple
Joe	4	3	3	3	13	Peach
					12.33	

#78 Adams County - Back Alley Bakery (Hastings) @ 10:15 AM - $4.00

	Filling	Crust	Visual	Taste	Total	Type
AJ	3	4	1	5	13	Coconut
Charlie	5	4	3	5	17	Sour Cream Raisin
Joe	5	5	4	4	18	Key Lime
					16	

#79 Clay County - Legacy Bar & Grill (Harvard) @ 11:10 AM - $2.50

	Filling	Crust	Visual	Taste	Total	Type
AJ	5	3	2	5	15	Triple Berry
Charlie	2	4	3	2	11	Apple
Joe	3	2	2	3	10	Triple Berry
					12	

#80 Fillmore County - Sister's Cafe (Geneva) @ 12:12 PM - $3.00

	Filling	Crust	Visual	Taste	Total	Type
AJ	3	2	2	3	10	Apple
Charlie	2	2	4	2	10	Pecan
Joe	3	3	3	3	12	Cherry
					10.67	

#81 Saline County - Wil-Bol Lanes (Wilber) @ 1:25 PM - $1.50 `BEST`

	Filling	Crust	Visual	Taste	Total	Type
AJ	3	3	3	2	11	Sour Cream Raisin
Charlie	4	3	3	4	14	Raspberry Apple
Joe	4	2	2	3	11	Peach
					12	

Kearney County

Sister's Café

Wil-Bol Lanes

Key Lime at Back Alley

Peach at Wil-Bol

AJ at Wil-Bol

Triple Berry at Legacy

Back Alley Bakery

LEG #15

THE BIG APPLE

8/21/20 - 8/22/20 ———————————— **395 Miles**

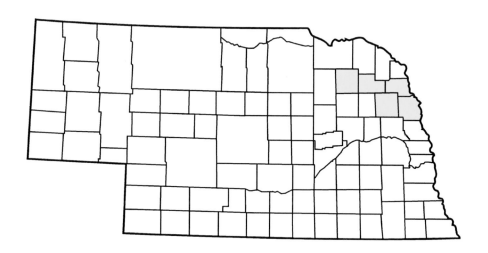

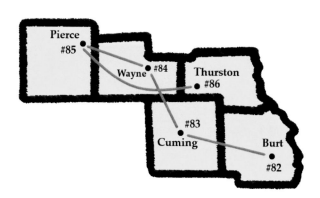

Burt County offered something different. We had heard the legend of a freezer full of Pies in a Tekamah church, where the honor system reigns and all you want is for the taking, assuming you leave payment. It was true. Everything we were told was true. Courtesy of the "Tekamah United Methodist Women" and the guidance of a local friend, we were led through the dark reaches of the lower level of Tekamah's United Methodist Church toward two full size freezers filled with Pies. Only one variety had yet to be tried during Pie-braska, therefore the Rhubarb Cream w/ Crumb Topping was chosen. This was also our first foray into baking a Pie entry ourselves, causing its fair share of stress, excitement and confusion. Kent, our local helping hand, provided his kitchen for us to get back on track, and took us to the local Chatterbox for a great dinner while our Pie baked. We tried to follow the "hint" on the baking instructions about cutting a hole in the foil that was to partially cover the Pie, giving us mixed results. Please forgive our sins United Methodist Women, we know not what we do. Nevertheless, the final result was more than satisfactory, and served as a great nightcap before heading out of town to set up camp.

After a poor night's sleep on the sandy beach of... some pond in Burt County covered with spiders, we made our way to the Beemer Cafe in Cuming County. We walked into dead silence and a table full of locals. The first words spoken were from an older gentleman addressing us with "Going golfing today?" followed by a chuckle. We didn't quite get the joke as we looked like anything but golfers, and he quickly followed that up with "Did you hear any fake news lately? Don't believe it." This caused more confusion, but we gave acknowledging nods, took our seats, and waited for the main course (Pie followed by bacon and eggs... and a cheeseburger).

In the town of Wayne in the county of the same name we met Vel, who has been running his own bakery there for just shy of 50 years. He was kind enough to prepare a Cherry Pie for us, and sat down for a chat while we ate. We discussed the changes in Lincoln that have occurred since the days when he called the capital city his stomping grounds, right before moving to Wayne for his new business venture. He was excited to be part of this strange thing we were doing and it was nice to hear his stories, like how much fun O St used to be in 1971... and how he got into zero trouble because of that fun. He also voiced his playful displeasure at our placement of Clarkson's Rhubarb Pie from two years prior as the still reigning champ. Before Vel sat down with us we were handed the full Pie in a box prepped to go, so we requested a knife and were invited to an open table to do the damage. The Ace of Diamonds was drawn and I got to work on cutting. Seconds later a yet-to-be-known local walked into Vel's and gave me an elbow nudge while asking under his breath "Are you serving Pie?" I laughed and said I sure was, and he promptly nudged me again and asked once more if I was serving Pie. Wonderful stuff.

Jerry's Hilltop Cafe (which uses a Randolph address, but is actually five miles to the southwest of town putting it barely inside the Pierce County line in case you're fact-checking) didn't offer anything revolutionary in ambience or experience, but offered one excellent piece of Pie and one very strange interaction. AJ had spoken to the Cafe before our arrival to make sure we could check them off our list, and walking in we seemed to all be on the same page. The greeter at the door said he remembered the conversation and followed that up with checking to see if they had any Pie. He then walked into the kitchen, out the back door, and immediately fled the scene in his truck. We were flooded with the usual worry we've encountered numerous times before in similar situations, but lucked out when the socially awkward teenage waiter informed us he had exactly three pieces left. I thought I lost the draw when I saw both Pecan pieces exit the Pie board, leaving me with the lone Apple. But as fate would have it, I soon ate the best Apple Pie of my life. A near perfect piece, finally allowing some hope for any future slice of this quintessential American classic. As we drove away with varying degrees of satisfaction, the doorman drove his truck back onto the lot.

Kathi's Kitchen in Pender was our final stop, making Thurston County the 86th notch on our belts. Kathi's is a made-to-order bakery just recently launched and operated out of her home, and she was more than willing to invite us into her backyard patio to enjoy the wonderful Peach Pie she donated to the cause. We talked of the times and of other must eat stops in Nebraska's northeast, as Kathi and Ken helped us brainstorm for our next statewide tour. The bow placed atop our visit was being interviewed by The Pender Times, their local paper. And so it was that another community got rocked by our earth-shattering story, allowing us once again to give the oh so stirring response to the burning question of why we do what we do... "we're not really sure."

QUOTES OUT OF CONTEXT

"When I say right go left... RIGHT!" - AJ

"Those bastards in Clarkson." - Vel

THINGS WE LEARNED

Sand isn't as comfortable to sleep on as you'd think.

Charlie really likes Kathi's pantry.

LEG #15 (8/21/20 - 8/22/20)

8/21/20 (1 stop)

#82 Burt County - United Methodist Church (Tekamah) @ 10:45 PM - $4.00

	Filling	Crust	Visual	Taste	Total	Type
AJ	5	3	3	4	15	Rhubarb Cream w/ Crumb Topping
Charlie	5	4	4	5	18	Rhubarb Cream w/ Crumb Topping
Joe	5	3	3	5	16	Rhubarb Cream w/ Crumb Topping
					16.33	

8/22/20 (4 stops)

#83 Cuming County - Beemer Cafe (Beemer) @ 8:40 AM - $3.00

	Filling	Crust	Visual	Taste	Total	Type
AJ	2	4	4	3	13	Sour Cream Raisin
Charlie	2	3	4	3	12	Sour Cream Raisin
Joe	3	4	4	3	14	Sour Cream Raisin
					13	

#84 Wayne County - Vel's Bakery (Wayne) @ 10:00 AM - $6.00

	Filling	Crust	Visual	Taste	Total	Type
AJ	3	4	3	3	13	Cherry
Charlie	3	4	3	2	12	Cherry
Joe	3	4	3	3	13	Cherry
					12.67	

#85 Pierce County - Jerry's Hilltop Cafe (Randolph) @ 10:54 AM - $2.99

	Filling	Crust	Visual	Taste	Total	Type
AJ	4	1	4	3	12	Pecan
Charlie	3	3	3	3	12	Pecan
Joe	5	5	4	5	19	Apple
					14.33	

#86 Thurston County - Kathi's Kitchen (Pender) @ 12:20 PM - $0.00 `BEST`

	Filling	Crust	Visual	Taste	Total	Type
AJ	5	4	5	4	18	Peach
Charlie	4	4	4	5	17	Peach
Joe	4	4	5	4	17	Peach
					17.33	

Wayne County

Vel's Bakery

Camping in Burt County

Waking up in a Bergman film

Enjoying our slices with Kathi

The freezer in Tekamah's Methodist Church

Apple at Jerry's Hilltop

Charlie gets to work in Kent's kitchen

LEG #16
FINAL STRETCH

10/10/20 ——————————————— **652 Miles**

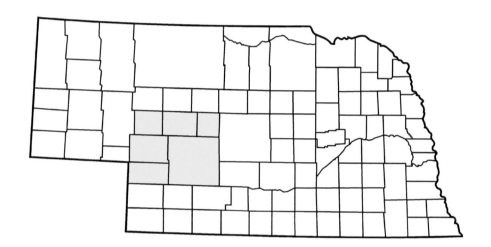

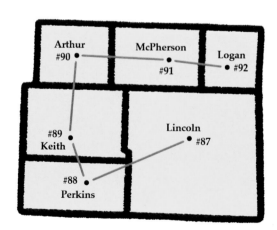

French press coffee, cockleburs and a game of Horse. What a day. Setting out on our final multi-Pie trek was bittersweet as we drove through the heart of Nebraska. AJ coaxed us into another night in a tent, this time going straight to the campground to rest up in preparation for a six Pie day. Nestling ourselves just inside the city limits of North Platte on a perfect night, it was enhanced further by the sweet serenading of what sounded like a dying wood flutist at 100 decibels, sounding off every 30 seconds. AJ swore it was an elk (which of course I questioned), but no verdict was settled on given the pitch black conditions. When morning hit I went for a pre-dawn walk, and while circling the nearby lake our resident wildlife expert was validated. I soon found myself inches away from the aforementioned elk, albeit on opposite sides of a fence. Now I can start my next Nebraska county checklist, where I get screamed at by something on four legs while looking it dead in the eyes from within five feet. One down, 92 to go. Thanks Lincoln County!

As we pushed on to more pressing matters, we made our way down the avenue to the Lincoln Highway Diner. They had many options, as well as many attentive waitresses after word got out what we were up to. When our plates were cleaned, Gina, a Nebraska resident of seven years, expressed her thanks and interest for our visit. She was born and raised in San Antonio, and proceeded to tell us how hard it was to find sour pickles in our state for her potato salad, and that she still hadn't gotten used to making enchiladas with flour tortillas ("They can only be made with corn!"). We recalled our favorites and where we'd been while Gina tried desperately and excitedly to remember her favorite Pie from the Village PieMaker. When she couldn't do it alone, she walked up to every table in the diner one at a time and asked, "What is that great kind with two fruits that they make?" While taking our picture, Gina said she would encourage her boys to do something like this. She missed the days of road tripping, reminiscing about her first time hitting South Dakota to see Pat Benatar. The lightness of the mood was tested when a woman sitting nearby got up to ask if Gina was our server. When we said she wasn't, her disgruntled reply coupled with an eye roll was, "She has a thing for guys." North Platte was a joy.

Once underway, our schedule got a bit tight in order to get where we needed during business hours, and that started with hitting the Madrid (pronounced "Mad-rid" by the locals) General Store in Perkins County promptly upon their opening. When Sharon turned on the open sign a bit early we happily strolled in. Not unlike many folks during the previous two and a half years, she seemed understandably surprised this was actually happening in spite of our earlier phone conversation requesting a Pie. She showered us with apologies for not being ready on the spot, then quickly eased our worries, happily hustling to bake the Pie in waiting for our potential appearance. We were able to fill the extra hour just down the road where a three-hooped basketball court was calling our name. AJ and I had made a recent trend of playing weekly games of Horse, and there was never a more perfect opportunity to hold a third person hostage to our version of the game, which we'd not so creatively dubbed "Crazy Horse." Its name originates from the insanely high degree of difficulty in every shot attempted. Remember the McDonald's commercials from the early 90's where Jordan and Bird took wild shots to try to win each others' fries? It's like that except we play for nothing, the shots are 10 times crazier, none of them go in, and we have no talent (or fries). Highlights included Charlie getting very dizzy on a merry-go-round, almost breaking some toddler-sized playground equipment with his back, and running into a fence post. We (AJ and I) had a blast.

Returning from our attempt to preemptively counteract the inevitably high caloric intake staring us in the face, we indulged ourselves in Sharon's Blueberry Pie. My card was drawn so I did the cutting and serving, causing great emotional distress from Charlie while he nursed his physical aches and pains. I was handed a tub full of ice cream, and by golly I was gonna use it if prodded, and that glob I put on Charlie's slice was enough for him to relegate an otherwise 20-point offering down to a 19. I only have myself to blame. We washed the excellence down with a fresh batch of French press coffee courtesy of the house, which even I tried because they were just so darned nice. I put in a scoop of vanilla ice cream when they weren't looking to see if it would help, which it didn't. This was not their fault, I was just born to hate coffee. It was a shame we had to rush to our next stop since the place had so much to see, and the staff and locals were amazing. We chatted on our way out the door with two women who were now considering eating cheesecake in every county. We gave them our blessing. "That's all we wanted," one of them said.

We continued on through a day where AJ ate Peach Pie almost exclusively. This included a park outing in Keith County's Ogallala, after we picked up a homemade Peach Berry from the Bittersweet Bakery mere seconds before closing time. The notable moment here would be when AJ served each of us a fully intact piece, and we collectively gazed into the Pie tin afterward only to find an extra crust. It's hard to explain how inexplicable and otherworldly the moment was, so I'll just leave it at that. We skipped over to the Bunkhouse in Arthur where I had my first helping of rocky mountain oysters (more Peach for AJ), and then into McPherson County's Tryon (guess what AJ had) where Shareen was kind enough to meet us at the Prairie Hills Cafe on her day off. Our final piece followed the same scenario when Wanda also opened the Dejowa Diner's doors in Stapleton for us on an otherwise closed day (this turned out to be a win-win, since we helped place the burden of putting up the chicken fence entirely on her husband). Where Wanda separated herself was by giving us two first time options to choose from in Logan County after 92 stops, which was rather impressive. She helped the Apple category finish with a strong entry thanks to her addition of cream cheese, all while having a Raspberry Blackberry in the other hand. Thanks Wanda, we'll see you next time for that game of cribbage!

Like the worst reality shows, our long trip home was both pathetic and riveting. In a desperate attempt to entertain ourselves, Charlie and I played a game of Heads/Tails (it's exactly what you think it is) to 100 where Charlie walloped me, putting the laws of probability very much in question. After that rousing start, we found that the only thing to get Charlie's heart rate above what he experiences while watching the Chicago Bears in the fourth quarter is to play the Alphabet Game in the dark (that's not just a colorful example, he actually checked his heart rate and it was 40 points higher than average). It's probably a good thing we're wrapping all this up.

QUOTES OUT OF CONTEXT

"He looks like a skier. Have you seen him ski?" - Lincoln Highway Diner patron referring to AJ

"Sod, sod, who has the sod?" - Charlie (singing)

Supernatural elements are at play in Ogallala.

Few things are funnier than Charlie's legs full of burs from the roadside.

Madrid General Store

Madrid, Perkins County

What Sharon Zimmerman, the manager of the General Store, loves about Madrid and the surrounding community is that she's more than just a number. Not dissimilar to much of the surrounding area, Perkins County and Madrid specifically is a farming community. This is what drew Sharon and her husband there, away from bigger city life in Wisconsin back in 1996. After working odd jobs, including at various cafes, Sharon eventually got pushed into the idea of running a store of her own. With the help of her brother and two sons, she was able to construct a new building in the winter of 2009, where the General Store opened on March 7th, 2010.

The seed for this idea goes back a few years earlier, when a friend of Sharon's ran a miniature prototype of the General Store out of her basement in Madrid. Selling miscellaneous items like books, dresses, gifts of all kinds and more, Sharon saw it as a model worth expanding upon and bringing to a larger audience. As she puts it, the "Mennonites bought the basement." Sharon wasted no time in starting her baking, seeing quickly that the idea of selling bulk foods was not going to take off all by itself in a community as small as Madrid. The baking became a staple of the new business model, and in the General Store's third year an addition was built to accommodate the newfound demand. In late 2019, a remodel was once again called for to include a new coffee shop as you walk through the front door. Through every incarnation, Sharon has made it a personal pledge to keep local sources the heartbeat of the store. They sell local honey, lotions, soaps and embroidered tea towels made by a neighbor, among other things. Sharon's Wisconsin connection remains intact, where she gets weekly orders of organic cheeses from a creamery she worked with years prior, as well as fresh maple syrup. When visiting it's easy to see why the General Store brings regular customers from far outside of Madrid and Perkins County.

Pleasures supplied by the General Store are simple for Sharon. She shared with me one of her favorite memories in her time there, when an older gentleman ordered a cup of breve coffee, and upon receiving it his eyes grew wide and he turned toward Sharon to deliver an emphatic thumbs up. There's also an old fashioned gumball machine in the store, which Sharon will happily supply the single penny it takes to operate if asked, an offer regularly taken advantage of by "kids of all ages," even if they collect social security. All this exists atop signature items of the General Store's like Caramel Pecan Cinnamon Rolls and delicious Blueberry Pie, featured in the weekly baking specials. You will also occasionally find Sharon's personal favorite Pie on the rack, a classic Cherry.

THE REGULAR:
Monica Poppe

Hailing from Grant, NE, just ten miles west of Madrid, Monica makes trips to the General Store a fixture in her schedule. Aside from the great Pies, rolls and coffee, Monica has been drawn to Madrid because of the great people. Although she is not Mennonite herself, most of her neighbors are, continually impressing her with their selflessness. When putting a roof on her house, three trucks pulled up with a crew ready to help re-shingle, an act done without warning and with nothing asked in return. "Those are the kind of people that run the General Store," says Monica. She also had a lot to say about Sharon's family at the store, like the fresh produce her son's greenhouses contribute, and how the coffee shop has been curated to perfection by her daughter, each tidbit indicating very clearly how personable and inclusive Sharon and everyone else is there. Monica tells me they're in tune with what people need, which keeps her coming back. When I asked how often she does, her excited reply was, "I go every week, whether I need something or not!"

LEG #16 (10/10/20)

#87 Lincoln County - Lincoln Highway Diner (North Platte) @ 8:45 AM - $3.29

	Filling	Crust	Visual	Taste	Total	Type
AJ	3	4	4	4	15	Peach
Charlie	2	3	4	2	11	Coconut Cream
Joe	4	3	4	4	15	Chocolate Peanut Butter
					13.67	

#88 Perkins County - Madrid General Store (Madrid) @ 11:04 AM (MST) - $3.75 `BEST`

	Filling	Crust	Visual	Taste	Total	Type
AJ	4	4	4	5	17	Blueberry (a la mode)
Charlie	5	5	4	5	19	Blueberry (a la mode)
Joe	4	5	4	4	17	Blueberry (a la mode)
					17.67	

#89 Keith County - Bittersweet Bakery (Ogallala) @ 12:00 PM (MST) - $5.20

	Filling	Crust	Visual	Taste	Total	Type
AJ	3	3	3	2	11	Peach Berry
Charlie	3	3	3	2	11	Peach Berry
Joe	4	3	4	2	13	Peach Berry
					11.67	

#90 Arthur County - Bunkhouse Bar & Grill (Arthur) @ 1:07 PM (MST) - $0.00

	Filling	Crust	Visual	Taste	Total	Type
AJ	4	4	3	4	15	Peach
Charlie	4	3	4	3	14	Peach
Joe	4	3	3	4	14	Peach
					14.33	

#91 McPherson County - Prairie Hills Cafe (Tryon) @ 3:31 PM - $2.00

	Filling	Crust	Visual	Taste	Total	Type
AJ	3	4	4	4	15	Peach
Charlie	3	2	4	2	11	Strawberry Rhubarb
Joe	3	4	3	4	14	Cherry
					13.33	

#92 Logan County - Dejowa Diner (Stapleton) @ 4:20 PM - $3.30

	Filling	Crust	Visual	Taste	Total	Type
AJ	5	3	4	5	17	Apple Cream Cheese
Charlie	4	3	4	4	15	Raspberry Blackberry
Joe	5	3	4	5	17	Apple Cream Cheese
					16.33	

Lincoln County

Bunkhouse Bar & Grill

Madrid General Store

A sticky situation

Apple Cream Cheese at Dejowa Diner

The other building in Arthur

Trick shot!

Mystery crust revealed!

LEG #17
HOME

10/23/20 ———————————————— **34 Miles**

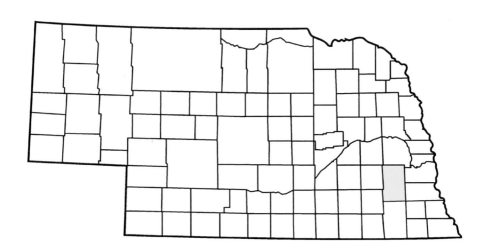

★
Lancaster
#93

We kicked around a lot of ideas for what our final stop in Lancaster County should be. We'd of course each had Pie countless times in the capital city we call home, but never together under the (un)official banner of Pie-braska. In the spirit of what we'd done 92 times prior, should we find a lesser known venue that's tucked away? Should we give the green light to a loved one to bake something where we'll have known good results, or revisit a regular stop we've had throughout our lives? Maybe we should make our own Pies and serve each other! After reaching no consensus in over two years, the weight of Pie-braska eventually made the decision for us. One thing we heard over and over from locals all around the state was how lucky we were to live in the same city that Stauffer's calls home. It seemed the perfect choice, and a nice tribute to a staple of our hometown whose reputation spreads far beyond the city limits.

Stauffer's Pies do hold noteworthy status, maintaining a reputation similar to the Village PieMaker. Even if you're not a Stauffer's regular, you don't have to live here long to come across their Pies at various catered events, or to enjoy them at other local establishments like the Hi-Way Diner. If you're noticing the mileage listed at the head of this chapter and wondering why our local stop put 34 miles on my car, it's because we had to first drive to the edge of Lancaster County to get our customary picture of the sign as we entered. If we have anything, we have principles.

As we strolled into Stauffer's on a Friday night, we were pleased to find a large Pie board with enough options that we could button this whole thing up with new varieties all around. Our first Apricot, Custard and Rhubarb Custard... and also our first piece of cake! In 92 counties leading up to Stauffer's, we had to practice leniency more than once with what some purists would surely not consider a traditional Pie. A crust made of Rice Krispies? Check. Apple Crisp disguised as Pie by slapping it on a ready made crust? Sure. Calling a Pie Root Beer Float? Why not? But when AJ's first choice of Boston Cream (from the Pie board mind you) arrived at our table, it was one we just couldn't allow, putting all of our hard work (eating Pie and having fun with our friends) in serious jeopardy. It was short on crust and heavy on cake, proving that we were clearly under-educated on what a Boston Cream Pie actually was beyond its entry in the Yoplait canon of flavors. We surely annoyed anyone inside of a 30 foot radius with our animated discussions about what was to be done, eventually deciding we would each double down. An unofficial rule we've had to adopt once or twice was that if any of us eats another piece of Pie at any given stop, the others had to do the same. Thus, Charlie and I ordered a second piece so AJ could tally his official 93rd entry. This put him in such a conflicted headspace that he forgot to take a nap on the way home (another first for Pie-braska).

So, after 974 days and over 8,000 miles, we had done it. What I will now retroactively refer to as my greatest college dream had been accomplished. What's next for the Pie Guys is hard to say. I've found since this started that I'm conditioned to want to stop the car any time I approach a county sign on the highway, with camera in hand and a stomach craving something that will have a negative impact on my health. Maybe we'll become Burrito Guys...

QUOTES OUT OF CONTEXT

"One ROOM boy!" - AJ
"This my ol' huntin' hat." - Vern

THINGS WE LEARNED

Boston Cream Pie needs a new name.

AJ will never feel complete.

LEG #17 (10/23/20)

#93 Lancaster County - Stauffer's Cafe & Pie Shoppe (Lincoln) @ 6:20 PM - $3.75

	Filling	Crust	Visual	Taste	Total	Type
AJ	2	3	4	2	11	Rhubarb Custard
Charlie	3	3	4	3	13	Custard
Joe	3	3	2	3	11	Apricot
					11.67	

It ends

Stauffer's Café

The almighty Pie board

Apricot at Stauffer's

ACKNOWLEDGMENTS

Many have left a special mark on Pie-braska while helping to make all of this possible. Whether you baked a Pie, helped us find one, or were just a good friend along the way, we thank you.

Ron Bartels
(The Red Cloud Chief)

Bob Beardslee

Cindy & Jeff Castor

Officer Clark
(Shelton Police Dept)

Carol Coleman

Dorothy Dexter

Sarah Disbrow

Judy & Brian Florian

Debbie Girard
(Polk County Clerk)

Aaron Grauer

Christee Haney
(Grant County Clerk)

Abbey Harig

Roger Holmes

Ray Kappel
(The Pawnee Republican)

Amber Karnes

Cindy Lange-Kubick
(Lincoln Journal Star)

Morgan Larson

Patti Lindgren
(Saunders County Clerk)

David Logan

Rich Lombardi

Tina Luz

Shirley Malone

Ryan Martinez

The McDaniel Family
(Cathy, Brent, Emily &
Anna)

Cindy McKillip

Matt Mehrhoff

Kay & Terry Mencl

Alysia Messersmith
(The Hayes Center
Times-Republican)

Sue Messersmith
(Hayes County Clerk)

Carrie Miller
(Nuckolls County Clerk)

Linda Moore

Lynn Nichols
(Wheeler County Clerk)

Neeli Noyd

Peter Osborne

Alice Osterman

Barb Paup

Liz Petsch
(Webster County Clerk)

Lisa Poff
(Buffalo County Clerk)

Monica Poppe

Martin Pugh

Chris Rasmussen

Liz Rasser

Tom Ristow

Kent Rogert

Bev Sack
(Howard County Clerk)

Nancy Scheer
(Madison County Clerk)

Sherry Schweitzer
(Seward County Clerk)

Matt Sehnert

Mataya Schwarz

Kathi & Ken Siebrandt

Dwain Sutton

Jeannie Tegtmeier

Darla Walther
(Frontier County Clerk)

Brett Wergin

Tom Wiemers

David Wishart

Nick Wolf

Randy Wolf

Danette Zarek
(Nance County Clerk)

Sharon Zimmerman

THE BREAKDOWN

AJ	13.51 avg.
Charlie	12.76 avg.
Joe	14.16 avg.

Avg	Pie	Scores
12.1	Apple	15 12 11 11 11 11 9 15 10 14 14 16 15 10 14
11	Apricot	11
13.27	Banana Cream	17 13 16 10 10 14 16 11 13 14 12
14.86	Blueberry	12 16 11 12 17 19 17
13.65	Candy	11 16 11 15 15 13 12 15 7 11 16 9 14 16 14
12	Cherry	8 9 9 12 12 13 13 12 8 11 11 11 17 10 13
13.07	Chocolate	9 9 14 13 15 20 17 19 11 9 7 12 17 9 15
14.4	Coconut	12 15 12 13 13 15 15 19 12 18 16 18 15 9 19
13	Custard	13
15.5	French Silk	15 16
17	Gooseberry	17
15.67	Key Lime	14 15 18
13.3	Lemon	13 18 12 9 16 11 15 14 13 12
14	Marionberry	14
12.38	Mixed Fruit	10 15 14 10 11 11 15 13
9.33	Mocha	8 9 11
15	Oatmeal	15
14.21	Peach	11 8 14 17 16 16 15 17 14 12 17 15 11 16 13
14.17	Pecan	14 19 18 11 14 16 11 17 12 15 13 13 17 16 15
12	Pumpkin	14 10 13 13 15 11 8 12 12
16.73	Rhubarb	19 15 19 18 20 15 18 15 18 16 11
14.71	Sour Cream Raisin	19 17 13 14 16 12 15 13 14 17 17 16 11 17 13
14.33	Strawberry	16 14 13
13.05	Strawberry Rhubarb	13 14 19 10 8 14 14 14 8 12 18 15 16 13 10

| 7 | 11 | 12 | 16 | 13 | 10 | 8 | 9 | 12 | 12 | 11 | 11 | 11 | 12 | 10 | 14 | 11 | 10 | 14 | 11 | 19 | 17 | 17 |

16	17
13	12	13	14

| 13 | 16 | 18 | 19 | 18 | 13 | 11 |

| 7 | 13 | 11 | 18 | 17 | 17 | 15 | 15 | 15 | 14 | 14 |

| 10 | 11 |

THE RECIPES

Toasted Coconut Pie
MADELINE'S CAFÈ & BAKERY

Prepare pie crust, pricking the bottom with a fork, lining with parchment or foil, and filling with pie-weights. Bake for 40-50 minutes, or until crust is golden brown. Allow to cool.

Spread 5 cups of Shredded Coconut and 1/2 cup of Pecans on baking sheet and bake for increments of 5 minutes, stirring between, until evenly golden brown. Remove from oven and set aside to cool.

In the stand mixer, beat 1 (8 oz) section of Cream Cheese, then stream in 1 (14 oz) can Sweetened Condensed Milk. Scrape the bowl and continue beating until a smooth custard-looking texture is formed. Scrape bowl again, then add in 3/4 bag of Whipped Topping and beat again until smooth and glossy.

Take your cooled pie shell, and spread about 3/4 cup layer of fluff on the bottom. Press about 3/4 cup of coconut into this layer, then generously drizzle with Caramel Sauce. Repeat this process as many times as you possibly can - ideally you would get 6 layers, but 4-5 is fine. No less than that though. Once you've used up all your fluff and coconut, make sure the pie is rounded off nicely, and cover in a final drench of caramel. Chill for at least 2 hours before serving.

SOUR CREAM PEACH PIE

"Jeannie's Place"

Clarice Tegtmeier

1 unbaked 9-inch pie crust
1 c. sour cream
2 T. flour
1 egg
$1/2$ c. sugar

$1/2$ tsp. salt
1 tsp. vanilla
2-3 c. sliced peaches or 1 (29-oz.) can, drained

Topping:

$2/3$ c. brown sugar
$1/4$ c. margarine or butter

$1/2$ c. flour
$1/2$ tsp. cinnamon

Blend sour cream, flour, egg, sugar, salt and vanilla. Add peaches. Pour into unbaked pie crust. Protect edge of crust with foil or a protector. Bake at 400° for 30 minutes or until set. Cut butter or margarine into other topping ingredients with fork or pastry blender. Sprinkle on top of baked pie. Return to oven for 15 or 20 minutes until bubbly. You can substitute partially cooked apples.

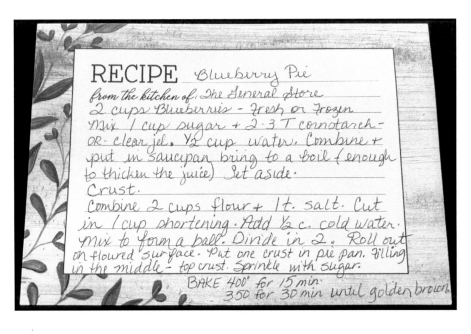

RECEIPE Blueberry Pie

from the kitchen of: The General Store

2 cups Blueberries - Fresh or Frozen
Mix 1 cup sugar + 2-3 T cornstarch - OR - clear jel. ½ cup water. Combine + put in saucepan bring to a boil (enough to thicken the juice) Set aside.

Crust.

Combine 2 cups flour + 1t. salt. Cut in 1 cup shortening. Add ½ c. cold water. Mix to form a ball. Divide in 2. Roll out on floured surface. Put one crust in pie pan. Filling in the middle - top crust. Sprinkle with sugar.

BAKE 400° for 15 min
350 for 30 min until golden brown.

Sweet Shoppe
Coconut Cream Pie

1 C. sugar
¼ c. cornstarch
2 tsp vanilla.
3 c milk
4 egg yolks

Cook till thick Add
½ C. or more coconut
Pour into baked Pie Crust.

Meringue

4 egg white
Sprinkle Cream of tarter
Beat til foamy
Add Sugar & Beat
¼ to ⅓ C sugar
Beat Till stiff
I use 4 or 6 egg
whites

Crust

2 cups all-purpose flour,
plus additional flour as needed
(up to 1/4 cup)

1/2 cup cake flour
(recommended: Soft As Silk)

3 tsp sifted powdered sugar

1/2 cup butter-flavored
shortening (recommended: Crisco)

1/4 cup salted butter

Pinch of salt

1 egg

2 tsp vinegar

1/4 cup ice cold water

Using 2 pastry blenders, blend the flours, sugar, shortening, butter and salt. Whisk the egg, vinegar and water in a 2-cup measure and pour over the dry ingredients incorporating all the liquid without overworking the dough. Toss the additional flour over the ball of dough and chill if possible. Divide the dough into 2 disks. Roll out 1 piece of dough to make a bottom crust. Place into a pie dish. Put dish in refrigerator to chill.

Preheat oven to 425 degrees F

Strawberry Rhubarb Pie
The Patriot Grill

Filling

2 1/2 cups chopped red rhubarb,
fresh

2 1/2 cups de-stemmed, washed
and cut strawberries (large pieces)

1 1/2 cups sugar (1 14 cups for
high altitude)

2 tbsp minute tapioca

1 tbsp all-purpose flour

1/2 tsp lemon zest

1/2 tsp ground cinnamon

1 tsp vanilla extract

3 tbsp butter, cubed small

1 egg white beaten with 1 tsp water

Large granule sugar

Mix the rhubarb, strawberries, sugar, tapioca, flour, zest and juice of lemon, dash of cinnamon, and vanilla. Mix well in a large bowl and pour out into chilled crust. Dot the top of the filling with the butter. Brush edges of pie crust with egg white wash. Roll out the other piece of dough and place over filling. Crimp to seal edges. Brush with egg white wash and garnish with large granule sugar. Collar with foil and bake at 425 degrees F for 15 minutes. Decrease temp to 375 degrees F and bake for an additional 45 to 50 minutes, or until the filling starts bubbling. Higher altitude will take 450 degrees F and 400 degrees F respectively. Also, you can use a pie bird for extra decor. Let cool before serving.

cool crust -
ill _____ with:
　1 C. cream whipped (sugar)
　Fold in 1 C. drained fruit.
Refrigerate over nite.
Strawberries, Raspberries

Sehnert's Fruit Meringue Pie

Fruit Meringue Pie
(Soda Crax Pie)

3 egg whites beaten stiff
add 1 C. sugar slowly
Fold In:
　12 ground up soda crax.
　1/4 tsp. Bk Pwd.
　1/2 C. pecans
　1 tsp. vanilla
Bake in Buttered Pie Tin 325°
　　　(over)　　25-30 min.

DIY!
COUNTY CHECKLIST

☐	Adams	☐	Frontier	☐	Nance
☐	Antelope	☐	Furnas	☐	Nemaha
☐	Arthur	☐	Gage	☐	Nuckolls
☐	Banner	☐	Garden	☐	Otoe
☐	Blaine	☐	Garfield	☐	Pawnee
☐	Boone	☐	Gosper	☐	Perkins
☐	Box Butte	☐	Grant	☐	Phelps
☐	Boyd	☐	Greeley	☐	Pierce
☐	Brown	☐	Hall	☐	Platte
☐	Buffalo	☐	Hamilton	☐	Polk
☐	Burt	☐	Harlan	☐	Red Willow
☐	Butler	☐	Hayes	☐	Richardson
☐	Cass	☐	Hitchcock	☐	Rock
☐	Cedar	☐	Holt	☐	Saline
☐	Chase	☐	Hooker	☐	Sarpy
☐	Cherry	☐	Howard	☐	Saunders
☐	Cheyenne	☐	Jefferson	☐	Scotts Bluff
☐	Clay	☐	Johnson	☐	Seward
☐	Colfax	☐	Kearney	☐	Sheridan
☐	Cuming	☐	Keith	☐	Sherman
☐	Custer	☐	Keya Paha	☐	Sioux
☐	Dakota	☐	Kimball	☐	Stanton
☐	Dawes	☐	Knox	☐	Thayer
☐	Dawson	☐	Lancaster	☐	Thomas
☐	Deuel	☐	Lincoln	☐	Thurston
☐	Dixon	☐	Logan	☐	Valley
☐	Dodge	☐	Loup	☐	Washington
☐	Douglas	☐	Madison	☐	Wayne
☐	Dundy	☐	McPherson	☐	Webster
☐	Fillmore	☐	Merrick	☐	Wheeler
☐	Franklin	☐	Morrill	☐	York